BATTLES FOR THE CHANNEL PORTS
LE HAVRE AND BOULOGNE
THEN AND NOW

BATTLES FOR THE CHANNEL PORTS
LE HAVRE AND BOULOGNE
THEN AND NOW

Edited by Daniel Taylor

An Imprint of Pen & Sword Books Ltd

Battles for the Channel Ports: Le Havre and Boulogne Then and Now
Copyright © After the Battle and Daniel Taylor, 2023

Published by After the Battle
An imprint of Pen & Sword Books Ltd
George House, Units 12 & 13, Beevor Street, Off Pontefract Road,
Barnsley, South Yorkshire, S71 1HN, England
Tel. 01226 734222
Fax. 01226 734438
Email: enquiries@pen-and-sword.co.uk
Website: **www.afterthebattle.com**
www.pen-and-sword.co.uk

Printed and bound in India by Replika Press Pvt. Ltd.

ISBN: 9781399031110

Commissioning Editor: Rob Green
Editor: Daniel Taylor
Design: SJmagic DESIGN SERVICES, India

Credits:
This book is based on two articles published in *After the Battle* magazine: 'Operation "Wellhit": The Capture of Boulogne' by Ian Galbraith (Issue 86, November 1994) and 'The Capture of Le Havre' by Karel Margry (Issue 139, February 2008).

Acknowledgements:
Publication of this book presents a rare opportunity to unite two fascinating yet neglected accounts of the fighting in Northwest Europe. Stranded between the Normandy Campaign and the 'Great Swan' advance through France and Belgium in the heady late summer of 1944, the fight for the Channel ports deserves to be better known. It is thanks to the extraordinary and dedicated work of Karel Margry and the late Ian Galbraith that this crucial episode can be brought to light.

I would also like to thank SJmagic Design Services, India, for creating the layout of this book.

Rob Green has, once again, been instrumental in supporting me during the editorial process. Additionally, a team of proof readers has checked and polished the work to ensure that the final version is readable, clear and accessible. On this occasion I would like to highlight the assistance of Joseph Taylor and Angus Taylor.

Daniel Taylor 2023.

Front Cover:
Above: A Humber scout car of the 141st RAC stands on the Rue Félix Faure, surrounded by recently liberated members of the French resistance. IWM BU 916
Below: Retracing the course of the battle the precise location was found west of the Fort de Tourneville, on the road's junction with Rue Begouen. The house on the right was No. 48 in 1944 but today it is No. 294.

Rear Cover:
Above: The Sherman Crab flail tanks and Churchill AVREs of 79th Armoured Division close in on Strongpoint 5 outside Le Havre. IWM BU 1193
Below: The intervening years have taken away almost all signs of military activity but the landscape vividly illustrates the hazards of carrying out the assault over open fields.

Any un-credited images are from the *After the Battle* Archives.

CONTENTS

FOREWORD 6

INTRODUCTION 8

OPERATION 'ASTONIA' – Le Havre 10
   The Assault Force 10
   The Defences 12
   The Plan 14
   Preparation 17
   10th September 19
      49th Division (Phase I) 19
      51st Division (Phase I) 39
   11th September 46
      49th Division (Phase II) 46
      49th Division (Phase III) 48
      51st Division (Phase III) 52
   12th September 54
   As the Dust Settles 66

OPERATION 'WELLHIT' – Boulogne 74
   The Defenders 78
   The Assault Force 83
   Bombing Support 85
   Softening-Up 85
   D-Day 86
   The Assault 90
   The End 106

AFTERMATH 121

THE CONTROVERSY 122

CONCLUSION 128

ORGANISATION TABLES 131

THE FUNNIES 135

BIBLIOGRAPHY 136

FOREWORD

'INFANTRY WINS BATTLES, LOGISTICS WINS WARS.' is an oft repeated quote usually attributed to General John J. Pershing, commander of the American Expeditionary Forces during the latter stages of the First World War. The sentiment very likely precedes him and still remains true today. This book deals with the phase of operations that created a profound supply headache for Allied military planners in the late summer of 1944 and looks at the attempt to alleviate the problem. Having broken out from the beachhead in Normandy the Allies had to cope with a rapidly expanding front line that was moving daily away from the bottleneck that was their sole avenue of replenishment – the invasion beaches. Most particularly, they were reliant on the single remaining artificial 'Mulberry' harbour across which almost every drop of fuel, every round of ammunition, and every ration pack had to pass. The key imperative, therefore, was to secure additional unloading facilities, ideally much closer to the battle line.

In its familiar then-and-now style, *After the Battle* presents a blow-by-blow account of this crucial, though neglected, phase of the

fighting in northwest Europe. The trials and tribulations of Canadian First Army, charged with capturing the channel ports, is contrasted with the precarious predicament forced on the German forces upon whom their defence was thrust.

Once again, we have taken a set of articles from *After the Battle's* back catalogue and reproduced them here in renewed and re-edited form with additional information for a new generation of readers. One interesting aspect of the source material in this instance is that the two main articles were created some time apart. The Boulogne story appeared in issue 86 which was published in 1994. The article was largely written and compiled by a then serving Police Officer, Ian Galbraith, who died in unfortunate circumstances in 1999. The Le Havre story comes from issue 139 and was written by the magazine's former editor, Karel Margry for publication in February 2008.

Some of the comparison photographs can, to a degree, look a little dated, although on one level this gives another insight into the passage of time. The locations have been checked so that the reader might visit the battlefield or, as an alternative, use geographical mapping software like Google Street View to get a current picture of the same location.

Daniel Taylor
April 2023

INTRODUCTION

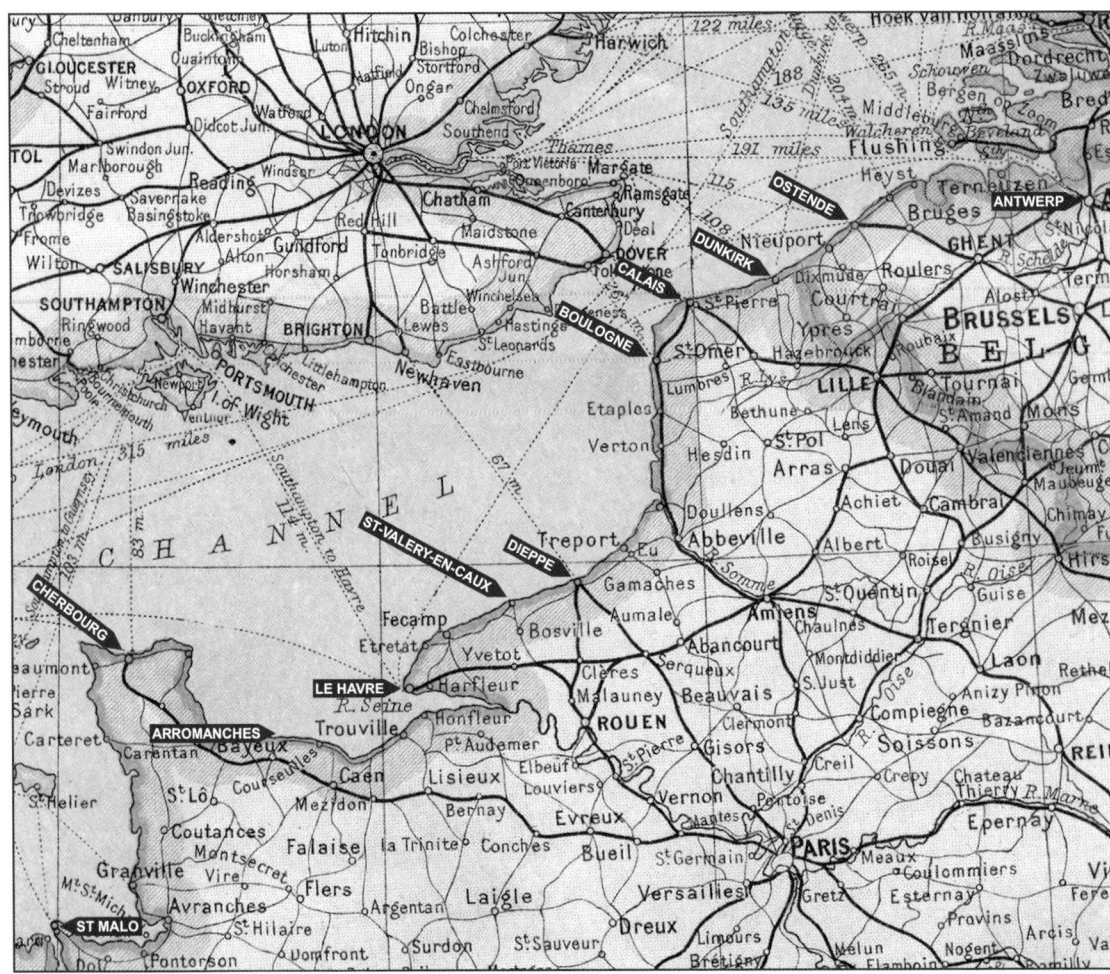

By the beginning of September 1944, the First Canadian Army was advancing along the Channel coast having bypassed and surrounded four major French ports: Le Havre, Boulogne, Calais and Dunkirk. These ports were urgently needed to alleviate the Allied supply problems and also to suppress the heavy cross-Channel guns around the Cap Gris-Nez that were still shelling the Dover area. Three separate operations were planned. Le Havre was overwhelmed in a neat 48-hour operation (code-named 'Astonia') between 10th and 12th September. Next came Boulogne (Operation 'Wellhit'), captured by the Canadian 3rd Division in a six-day operation from 17th September to the 22nd. After that it was the turn of Calais and the cross-Channel guns at Cap Gris-Nez (Operation 'Undergo'), reduced by the 3rd Canadian Division between 25th September and 1st October. Dunkirk, first invested by the 2nd Canadian Division, was not attacked. Field Marshal Montgomery had decided on 14th September that the town was to be merely contained. Its German garrison held out until the end of the war, surrendering on 9th May, 1945.

BY THE FIRST WEEK of September 1944, the Allied armies were sweeping north and east across France and into Belgium after their break-out from the Normandy bridgehead. In doing so, they bypassed and isolated the Channel ports of Le Havre, Boulogne, Calais and Dunkirk. During the next phase of the campaign the Allies had to work out a way to capture the ports in order to alleviate their growing logistical problems. Now some way behind the new battlefront, each of these ports had been declared a 'Festung' by Adolf Hitler himself and were being prepared for a vigorous defence in order that they would be denied to the Allies. At least, that's how they would have appeared from outside. The Germans who remained were formed as garrisons in each port and provision was made so that they could potentially hold out for months. Each was provided with a Fortress Commander, though the role tended to be allocated to anyone of suitable rank, rather than to officers with any recognised competence in this form of defensive battle. As will be shown, their understanding of the instruction to fight to the last was also to be interpreted differently by each of the commanders.

From the Allied point of view, the supply route now stretched hundreds of miles on a round trip from the invasion beaches almost to the German border and back. Methods had to be found to maintain the momentum of the pursuit. If these ports could be captured quickly, without serious damage to the harbour installations, the pressure on the Allied supply lines would be reduced. In order to guarantee a quick and successful assault, however, it would be necessary to compromise the safety of the French civilians past whom any attack would have to pass.

This account concentrates on the assaults on Le Havre – Operation Astonia – and Boulogne – Operation Wellhit. At all levels these attacks demonstrate the rigours of ground attack against prepared positions whilst highlighting a compelling series of decisions by senior commanders with far reaching consequences. The assault itself presented a perilous leap into the unknown. The troops were tasked with unpicking complex defensive positions nestled between French villages and in French towns. The airmen were compelled to press home attacks where the consequential loss of French lives would have been quite apparent. For the commanders, they had to weigh the moral ambiguity of the operation as they made decisions that effectively pitted the lives of those awaiting liberation against those of their own men. This was the stark choice of the decision makers as they evaluated the use of strategic bombers to achieve tactical goals. The rift created between Army and Air Force had the potential to severely strain the relationship between the two branches of the liberation force.

OPERATION 'ASTONIA'

Le Havre

THE ASSAULT FORCE

The task of capturing the Channel ports had been given to Canadian First Army, commanded by Lieutenant-General Henry Crerar. The Canadians had captured Dieppe and Ostend without a fight, but expected a heavy battle for the other ports. Since his resources were limited, Crerar decided that he would have to take each fortress in turn. The first to be assaulted was Le Havre, the great ocean port at the mouth of the Seine, and the task of reducing it was assigned to Lieutenant-General Sir John Crocker's British I Corps. SHAEF had allotted this seaport to the maintenance of the American armies. Thus a British corps under Canadian command would assault a port, the product of which was destined for American use.

British I Corps, composed of the 49th (West Riding) Division and 51st (Highland) Division, had crossed the Seine on 1st September, and leading elements of the 49th Division made contact with Le Havre's perimeter defences on the evening of the 2nd. It soon became clear that the port was garrisoned and that the Germans intended to offer a strong defence.

General Crocker now judged that a full-scale set-piece attack, with strong support by heavy bombers, naval gun-fire, artillery and special armoured equipment, would be necessary to reduce the defences. Obtaining and co-ordinating these various resources took time, and so a pause was made which meant that the assault could not be undertaken for over a week. As a first measure, the 51st Division, which had liberated St Valéry-en-Caux – site of its gallant defeat in 1940 – without difficulty on 2nd September, was ordered to move down the coast and take over the northern sector of the Le Havre perimeter, on the right of the 49th Division.

Le Havre lies at the entrance to the Seine estuary, along the river's northern bank. A fishing settlement since Roman times, its history as an ocean port began in 1517 when King François I set out to construct a new port city to replace the ancient harbours of Honfleur and Harfleur, whose utility had decreased due to silting. It had long been a city of much commercial and military significance and had figured prominently in the old Anglo-French wars, the British having bombarded it in 1694, 1759, 1794 and 1795. Later kings extended the harbour adding fortifications and Vauban greatly enlarged its capacity. By 1939 it was the second-largest port of France second only to Marseilles. A deep-water harbour, predominant in the American and colonial trade, it could accommodate the largest vessels afloat. The port comprised 15 basins in the harbour, the oldest of which dated back to 1669. Two of the basins were tidal, the other thirteen being wet docks, in total providing 22 kilometres of quays, equipped with 241 cranes and 27 special lifting appliances for grain, coal, timber, bananas, etc. with a daily capacity of 20,000 tons. Facilities included 29 floating cranes, seven dry docks, three floating docks and three petroleum wharves. The chief docks were the Bassin Bellot and the Bassin de l'Eure. The Canal de Tancarville, by which river boats unable to negotiate the Seine estuary can reach the port direct, enters the harbour by the latter basin. The city's industries included three shipbuilding yards, a Schneider motor and Diesel engines plant, two aircraft factories and many smaller chemical, engineering and metallurgical firms. The city itself is built at two distinct levels: the northern half lies on a fairly high escarpment while the lower parts of the city – the docks and the city centre – are along the Seine estuary. By September 1944, some 60,000 of the peacetime population of over 160,000 remained in the city, the rest having been forced out by German evacuation orders or fled as refugees from Allied bombing.

THE DEFENCES

Situated at the end of a peninsula, Le Havre had considerable natural strength. It was protected by water on three sides: on the west by the sea, on the south by the Seine estuary and the Tancarville Canal, and on the east by the deep valley of the Lézarde river, which the Germans had flooded to make it impassable. Consequently, the only approach to the town was from the north but this terrain was overlooked by high ground at Octeville-sur-Mer.

One of the strongest fortresses of the Atlantic Wall, Le Havre had been prepared for defence for five years. However, although the city was heavily fortified against naval attack, the landward defences were incomplete. A defensive line ran west of, and roughly parallel with the River Lézarde, turning west at Montivilliers to reach the coast by way of Dondenéville and Octeville. Considering this northern sector the weakest part of the front, the Germans had barred it with a deep, though not fully continuous, anti-tank ditch coupled with extensive minefields and barbed wire. Behind the ditch there were a number of strongpoints, each held by company-size units with concreted dugouts, machine guns, 8.8cm guns as well as other anti-tank guns.

In the town itself were two large forts – the Fort de Ste Adresse and the Fort de Tourneville (the old fort of Sanvic) – and many road-blocks, pillboxes and fortified houses, together with flak and anti-tank guns. The German garrison lacked a mobile reserve of tanks and self-propelled guns but was well equipped with artillery. The defenses included 35 coastal guns, most of which could fire only seaward and which included one 380mm and two 170mm guns in the Grand Clos battery three kilometres north of the city. For regular artillery, there were 44 medium and field guns and 32 anti-aircraft guns.

Le Havre had been designated a Festung (Fortress) in January 1944, one of 12 coastal installations selected by Hitler to be defended to the last in order to deny their use to the enemy. Fortress Le Havre had been commanded since mid-August by Oberst Eberhard Wildermuth, not a regular soldier but an officer of wide experience. Fifty-five years old, a bank director in civilian life, he had seen service in France, Russia and Italy before being appointed Festungskommandant of Le Havre, where he arrived on 14th August. Like all Fortress Commanders, Wildermuth had had personal orders from Hitler to demolish the harbour facilities and defend Le Havre to the last man.

Oberst Eberhard Wildermuth, Festungskommandant of Le Havre. Born in Stuttgart on 23rd October, 1890, Wildermuth fought in the First World War, being wounded twice. Between the wars, after commanding a Freikorps battalion until 1921, he completed his law studies in order of qualify to become a director of the Deutsche Bau und Bodenbank in Berlin in 1928. A reserve Major, he was called up in 1939 to lead the II. Bataillon of Infanterie-Regiment 272 of the 93. Infanterie-Division, earning the Ritterkreuz for actions during the attack on the Maginot Line in 1940. From July 1941, he served with the 717. Infanterie-Division in Serbia in anti-partisan operations. Promoted to Oberstleutnant in December 1941, he was given command of Infanterie-Regiment 371 of the 161. Infanterie-Division, fighting with Heeresgruppe Mitte at Rzhev on the upper Volga in Russia until September 1942. Released due to combat fatigue, he then spent time recovering in hospital until February 1943. The following May, promoted to Oberst, he was given command of Grenadier-Regiment 578 of the 305. Infanterie-Division, first on the Côte d'Azur, and then from August 1943 on the Italian front. After heavy combat on the Volturno and Sangro rivers, and another sojourn recuperating in hospital, he was assigned to command the coastal defence sector of Venice. On 12th August, 1944, he was transferred to Heeresgruppe B in France and appointed Fortress Commander of Le Havre two days later. After the war, released by the British in July 1946, he joined the Liberal Freie Demokratische Partei and became Minister of Housing in the West German government (1949-52). He died on 9th March, 1952. (BURKHARD WILDERMUTH)

The strength of the garrison was about 11,000 – Allied intelligence under-estimated it at 8,700. However, this figure included 4,000 artillery and flak personnel, and some 1,300 naval personnel of doubtful fighting value. A total of around 5,500 infantry troops were available, organised into six battalions of variable quality: Füsilier-Bataillon 226 and the I. and II. Bataillon of Grenadier-Regiment 1041 of the 226. Infanterie-Division; the III. Bataillon of Grenadier-Regiment 936 of the 245. Infanterie-Division; the III. Bataillon of Sicherungsregiment 5; and Festungs-Stamm-Abteilung 81, the latter a permanent fortress unit. The artillery units included the personnel of Heeres-Küsten-Artillerie-Regiment 1254 and Marine-Artillerie-Abteilung 226, which manned the Army and Navy coastal batteries, and of schwere Flak-Abteilung 193, which operated the AA batteries in and around the centre of Le Havre. The naval personnel comprised what remained of the Kriegsmarine patrol boat, torpedo boat and minesweeping flotillas that had been stationed at Le Havre. The garrison was amply stocked with food and ammunition, enough to last for three months.

On 20th August, Wildermuth ordered a general evacuation of the entire civilian population. The townspeople, still with bad memories of the exodus of 1940 and expecting liberation to arrive any day, were naturally reluctant to leave their homes. The local Resistance called on them to disobey the German decree. As a result, few left the city. The order was repeated on 31st August, but with little effect. Meanwhile, the Germans began the systematic demolition of the port facilities.

THE PLAN

Meanwhile, General Crocker and his staff were planning the operation to capture the city. It was clear to both sides that any attack had to be made from the north. Crocker, however, avoided the obvious line of approach and chose the indirect, more unexpected north-east corner of the German perimeter. The terrain here, west of the Lézarde river, is characterised by two high-ground plateaus, separated from each other by the Fontaine river (a tributary of the Lézarde). The northern plateau lies south-west of Montivilliers and was bisected by the German anti-tank ditch. The southern plateau is partly covered by the Forêt de Montgeon, which lies by the northern outskirts of Le Havre and stretches east as far as the escarpment that overlooks Harfleur and the lower parts of the city along the Seine estuary.

General Crocker decided to launch his corps with the 49th Division, supported by the 34th Tank Brigade, on the left and the 51st Division, with the 33rd Armoured Brigade, on the right. Owing to the nature of the outer defences it was necessary for both divisions to attack virtually at the same point – the narrow sector between the villages of Montivilliers and Fontaine-la-Mallet – and in order to meet this situation, the 49th Division would make its assault by day and the 51st Division by night.

The final plan of attack for the two divisions – code-named Operation 'Astonia' – was in four parts: the first phase called for the 56th Brigade of the 49th Division to breach the German outer defences and capture the northern plateau while seizing a bridgehead on the southern plateau. The second phase would see the 51st Division secure a base further west, on the north edge of the Forêt de Montgeon, while the 147th Brigade of the 49th Division would follow up through the gap made by 56th Brigade and seize the southern plateau. In the third phase the 146th Brigade of the 49th Division would launch a separate attack from east of the Lézarde and clear all the enemy up to Harfleur. During that same phase the Highland Division would wheel right towards the sea, destroy fortified areas and gun batteries south of Octeville – at Les Monts-Trottins, Févretot, Ste Catherine, Bléville and Cap de la Hève – and secure dominating ground on the north-western outskirts of Le Havre itself. The final phase would see both divisions attacking into the city itself.

To carry out the assault the two infantry divisions were greatly strengthened by special armour provided by the British

79th Armoured Division: Sherman Crabs (mine-sweeping flail tanks) from the 22nd Dragoons and the 1st Lothians and Border Yeomanry; Churchill Crocodiles (flame-throwing tanks) of the 141st Battalion, Royal Armoured Corps; Kangaroos (armoured personnel carriers) operated by the 1st Canadian APC Squadron;

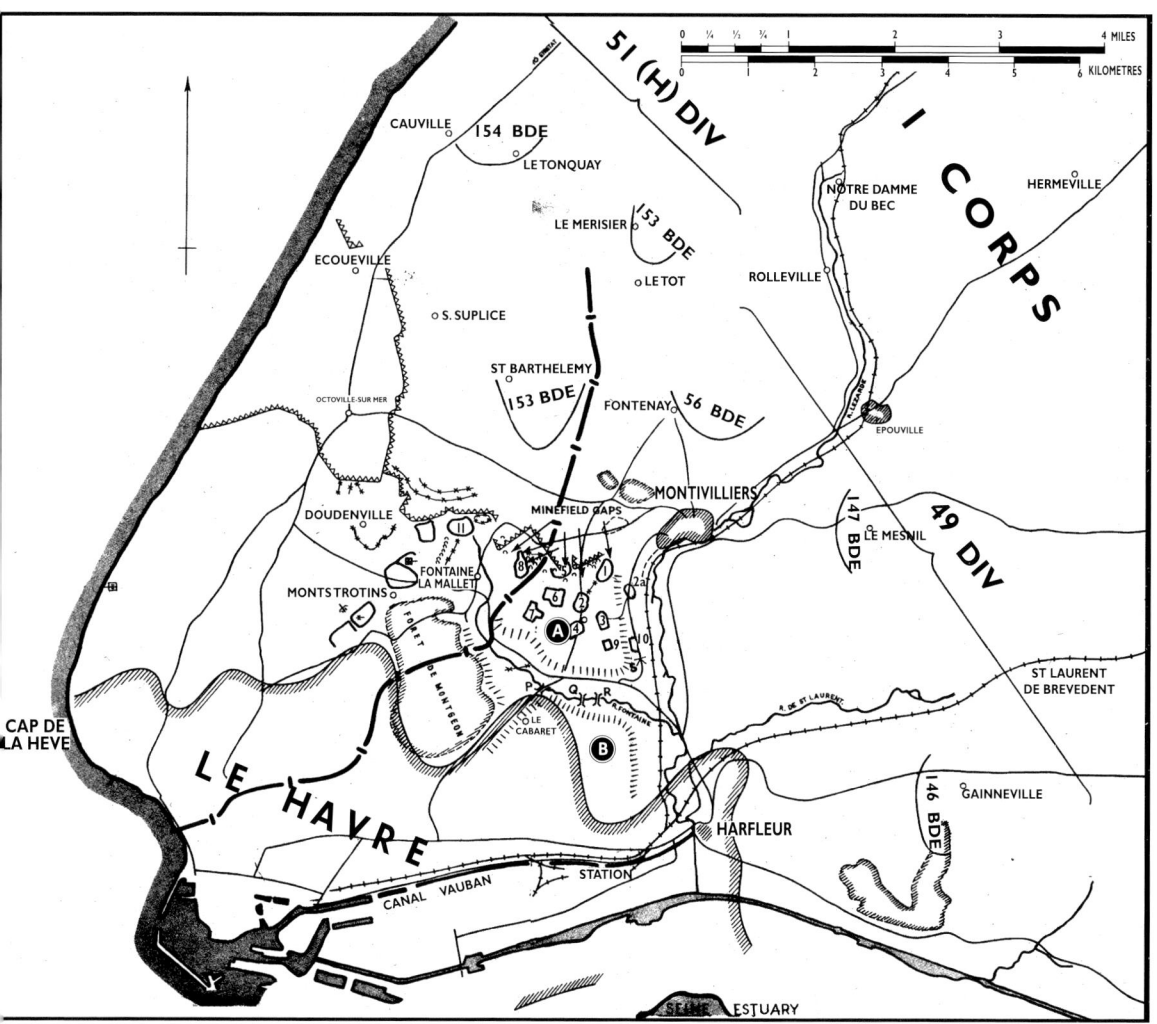

The outline plan for Operation 'Astonia'. The attack on the Le Havre perimeter would be launched from the north-east and begin with the 56th Brigade of the 49th Division opening up breaches through the German minefield and anti-tank ditch in order to capture the German strongpoints on the northern plateau (marked 'A' on the map). The strongpoints to be captured had been numbered 1 to 11 by the planners. Next, the 152nd Brigade of the 51st Division would widen the gap on the immediate right of the 49th Division and fan out towards the west to neutralise the enemy gun batteries around Monts-Trottins and along the coast. At the same time, the 49th Division's 147th Brigade would cross the Fontaine river and clear the southern plateau (marked 'B'). In a third phase, the 146th Brigade would launch an attack from the east, through Harfleur, opening up a new line of advance. In the final phase, both divisions would drive down into the city.

and Churchill AVREs (Assault Vehicles Royal Engineers) of the 16th, 222nd, 284th and 617th Assault Squadrons, RE. AVREs were armed with a powerful Petard spigot mortar that could throw 40lb projectiles ('flying dustbins') against concrete fortifications but could also carry or tow a number of special devices: an SBG assault bridge to cross anti-tank ditches; fascines (larges bundles of chestnut paling) to fill up anti-tank ditches; a 'Snake' (lengths of explosive-filled pipe) to detonate mines and blow a path through barbed-wire obstacles; armoured sledges, etc.

The main task of the specialised armour was to create breaches in the minefields and crossings over the anti-tank ditch. The breaches would all be made on the narrow front between Montivilliers and Fontaine-la-Mallet where there were two gaps in the anti-tank ditch – one 400, the other 200 yards wide – and on these convenient crossings the assault would be directed. It was decided to have 11 gapping teams that would create as many lanes through the minefields – eight in the 49th Division's sector and three in that of the 51st Division. The three breaches for the 51st Division were code-named 'Gin' (Lane 1), 'Rum' (Lane 2) and 'Ale' (Lane 3) respectively. The teams for the 49th Division would make three multi-lane breaches, code-named 'Laura' (Lanes 4-6) 'Hazel' (Lanes 7-9) and 'Mary' (Lanes 10-11). As soon as the gapping teams had opened up a mine-free path, the infantry and their supporting armour would pass through and assault the enemy strongholds.

The gapping teams all comprised a mixture of special armour and infantry tanks, usually a troop of five mine-clearing Crabs, a troop of six AVREs – one carrying an assault bridge, one pulling a Snake, three carrying a fascine –, a troop of three flame-throwing Crocodiles and a troop of Churchill or Sherman gun tanks. However, the composition and order of march of each team varied according to the problems to be mastered. At gaps 'Gin', 'Rum' and 'Ale', the minefields only began on the far side of the anti-tank ditch, so the teams here would be led by the AVREs to first bridge or fill in the ditch and the Flails would come after. At 'Laura', 'Mary' and 'Hazel', where the minefield preceded the ditch, the Flails would go in the lead with the AVREs, Crocodiles and gun tanks following. At 'Laura' and 'Mary' there was no anti-tank ditch to cross, so the teams here went in without bridge-laying or fascine-carrying AVREs. The centre lane of 'Hazel' (Lane 8) was a surfaced road believed to be clear of mines, so the team here went in without mine-clearing Crabs leading the way. All lanes were to be 24 feet wide, except Lane 8 which was to be the width of the existing road.

PREPARATION

Before the assault, the German defences were subjected to a series of co-ordinated naval and air bombardments, I Corps having been authorised to communicate directly with RAF Bomber Command and the Royal Navy. On 5th September, the monitor HMS Erebus engaged the coastal defences with her two 15-inch guns but was herself hit by the Grand Clos battery and had to temporarily withdraw to Portsmouth for repairs. That same day, Bomber Command began its attacks with a daylight raid, 348 aircraft in total – 313 Lancasters, 30 Mosquitos and five Stirlings of Nos. 1, 3 and 8 Groups – dropping 1,820 tons of high explosive and 30,000 incendiaries on the dock area and gun positions. The attack completely destroyed Le Havre's inner city. The entire part between the Basin de Commerce and the sea – a square mile containing the town hall, post office, grand theatre, two municipal museums and the churches of Notre-Dame, St Michel and St Joseph – was reduced to a wasteland of ruins. Civilian casualties were horrendous, 781 being killed and 289 missing. Thousands lost their homes.

An aerial oblique showing Le Havre on 5th September. The centre of the town is being erased from the map by 1,860 tons of high explosive and incendiaries dropped by 348 aircraft of Bomber Command. Although the bombing was accurate, it is said to have inflicted little damage on the Germans.

The bombers returned the following evening (6th September), 344 aircraft dropping another 1,500 tons on the defence works and ammunition depots on the southern plateau. Again the civilian population suffered badly: 655 were killed and ten were reported missing. One single bomb hit the southern end of the Jenner Tunnel, the traffic underpass then under construction between the upper and lower city, and blocked the entrance, asphyxiating 319 French civilians that had taken refuge there. Only seven of whom could be dug out and rescued.

On the 8th there was another daylight attack by 333 bombers on the north-western part of town. The weather was bad with a low cloud base and only 109 aircraft released their bomb load, putting down another 535 tons. That same day, Erebus returned for a second bombardment but was again hit.

A strong air attack mounted on the 9th was also frustrated by cloudy weather, all 272 despatched bombers being ordered back by the Master Bomber due to bad visibility before any bombs were dropped.

In all, before the ground assault was unleashed, Bomber Command had dropped some 4,000 tons of bombs on Le Havre. The massive raids, accurately carried out, caused comparatively few casualties among the German troops, safe in their deep underground shelters, but the French civilian population suffered grievously, a total of 2,053 being killed.

In the week before the assault, the British finalised their preparations. Numerous planning conferences were held at corps, division, brigade and battalion level. Patrols scouted out the enemy defences, minefields and obstacles. French resistance fighters and evacuees brought invaluable information on the enemy's disposition. Scale models of the town and its pillbox defences were made and studied by all ranks. Officers studied air photographs and defence overprints, which were extremely detailed. The armoured gapping teams held rehearsals and most infantry battalions carried out street-fighting exercises.

The main worry was the weather – for several days in advance of the attack it rained practically without let-up. The deluge turned the pastures over which the attack had to pass into a bog. The near constant overcast compounded the problems for the bombing programme, which was inevitably interrupted, as noted above. On 7th September General Crocker was forced to postpone the assault by 24 hours due to the bad weather. Instead of 9th September, D-Day was to be the 10th. Commanders realised that the sodden ground would prove a serious handicap to the armour, particularly the Flails, but no further postponement of the attack could be made. H-Hour was set at 1745-hrs – a late starting time, leaving only some four hours of daylight, though the unusual hour would enhance surprise. On the evening of 9th September, the British sent the German garrison another surrender ultimatum but Oberst Wildermuth again rejected it.

10th SEPTEMBER

49th DIVISION (Phase I)

Sunday, 10th September, dawned fine and sunny, with an easterly wind that promised to dry the heavy clay soil just enough to make tank operations viable. The day's activities began with an attack by 65 aircraft of Bomber Command on the Grand Clos battery. Erebus returned, this time together with the battleship HMS Warspite, to bombard casemated guns on Le Havre's perimeter defences. The Grand Clos battery again fired back but this time scored no hits. Warspite fired 304 rounds, which reportedly finally silenced the Grand Clos battery. Erebus was credited with scoring 30 hits out of about 130 rounds.

The week-long air attack on the city reached its climax with a three-phase bomber raid on the main defensive positions, which began at 1645-hrs. The first wave dropped its load on the western defence area of Le Havre, the second on the belt of defences around Octeville and on the northern plateau, and the third on the southern plateau. In all, 992 aircraft – 521 Lancasters, 426 Halifaxes and 45 Mosquitos – dropped 4,719 tons of explosive on eight different German strongpoints, each target being separately marked by the Pathfinders. The raid, an impressive display of Allied aerial might, had a heartening effect on the morale of the British troops, who had a grandstand view of it, but again caused relatively few personnel losses among the well-protected German troops. The main positive effect was the breakdown of communications which prevented the German commanders from being kept informed on what was going on. The principal victim was again the civilian population of Le Havre and the outlying villages.

Meanwhile, a heavy counter-battery shoot by the divisional artilleries of I Corps – six field regiments – supplemented by six medium and two heavy regiments of the 4th and 9th Army Group, Royal Artillery, massed in a semi-circle around Le Havre, reduced the enemy redoubts even further. The artillery programme included barrages of HE fire by the tanks of several of the participating armoured regiments and counter-flak fire (known as 'Apple-Pie') during the bomber operations.

At 1745-hrs, immediately after the cessation of the bombing of the northern plateau, the 49th Division began the ground assault. As the armoured gapping teams moved out of the dead ground of their forming-up points and ran for the start line – the lateral road from Montivilliers to Fontaine-la-Mallet that ran parallel with the edge of the minefield – the tank crews saw before them a shallow basin of open fields, its far slope rising to the bomb-shattered copses that masked the enemy strongpoints. All was quiet on the enemy side.

At 1815-hrs, the gapping teams moved off to open up the eight lanes for the 56th Brigade (Brigadier Maurice Ekins). On the right, A Squadron, 22nd Dragoons, their flails whirling and flogging the ground, began to cut open the three lanes of the 'Laura' gap, which

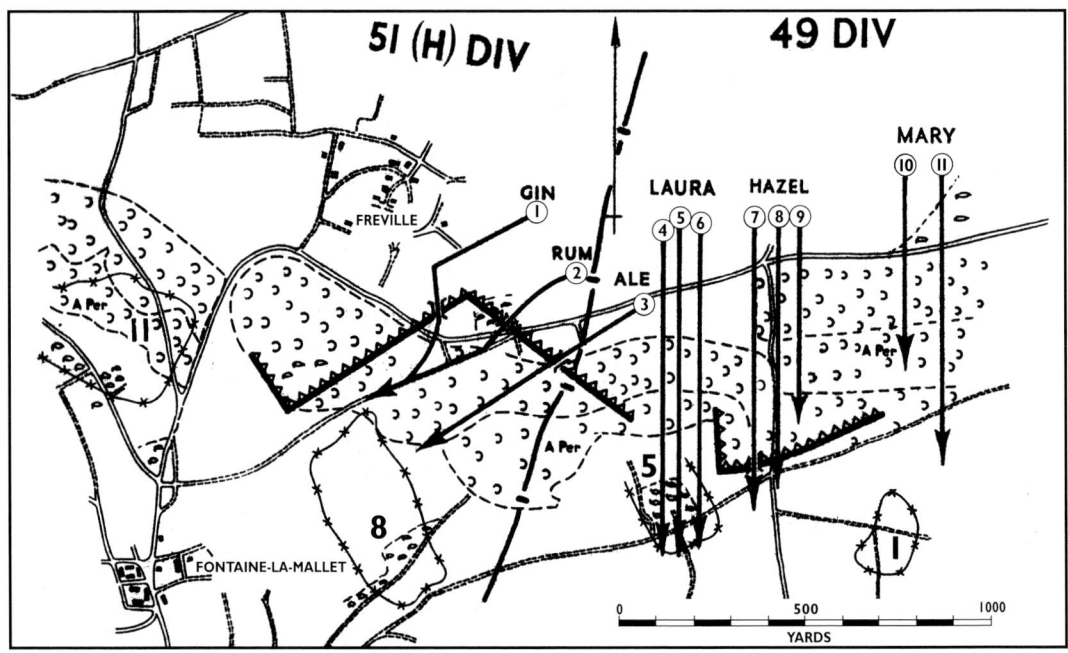

The assault area in the north-east comprised a very narrow sector of some 1,500 yards between the towns of Montivilliers and Fontaine-la-Mallet and was chosen due to the two gaps in the anti-tank ditch at this point. The plan was to open eleven lanes through the minefield and (where necessary) across the anti-tank ditch – three for the 51st Division and eight for the 49th Division. The 51st Division had single-lane breaches that were code-named 'Gin' (Lane 1), 'Rum' (Lane 2) and 'Ale' (Lane 3). The lanes for the 49th Division were grouped in three breaches that were code-named 'Laura' (Lanes 4-6), 'Hazel' (Lanes 7-9) and 'Mary' (Lanes 10 & 11), individual lanes within each breach being referred to as 'Red', 'White' and 'Green'. Thus Lane 4 was 'Laura Red', Lane 5 'Laura White', etc. A gapping team composed of specialised armour would open up each of the eleven lanes. In the event, not all teams achieved a breakthrough or followed the prescribed course. The arrows show the actual routes.

led straight to Strongpoint 5 directly ahead (the 'Astonia' planners had numbered the strongpoints on the northern plateau 1 to 11). The Crabs had to turn their gun turrets to the rear during flailing but they received covering fire from the Churchills of the 7th Royal Tanks. The assault began well but when the Crabs had got halfway down the minefield they came under fire from a hitherto undiscovered enemy anti-tank gun sited in the wooded depression on the right flank. Part of Strongpoint 8 (a 51st Division objective) and well concealed, it proved extremely difficult to locate. Smoke was quickly put down, but casualties from its deadly fire were inevitable. Also, owing to 'heavy' going in the soft ground and consequent loss of flailing power, Crabs started to blow up on mines.

The troop under 2nd Lieutenant Charles Neil flailing on the extreme right of 'Laura' (Lane 4) bore the brunt of the enemy cross-fire. The leading Crab was hit, its turret was blown off and

Crocodile flame-throwers of A Squadron of the 141st RAC, their trailers full of fuel, waiting to go into action with the 49th Division. On the right (wearing a long coat), talking to one of the crews, is Major-General Percy Hobart, commander of the 79th Armoured Division, to which the 141st RAC were attached. Brigadier Nigel Duncan, who with Headquarters 30th Armoured Brigade commanded all units of the 79th Armoured Division at Le Havre, stands second from right.

Sunday, 10th September, 1944 – D-Day for Operation 'Astonia'. In the early afternoon, Sergeant Albert Wilkes of No.5 Army Film and Photo Unit (AFPU) pictured Churchills of the 7th Royal Tank Regiment waiting to go into action in the Forming-Up Point in the valley just north-west of Montivilliers. The 7th Royal Tanks were assigned to support the 56th Brigade, A Squadron being with the 2nd Essex, B Squadron with the 2nd Gloucesters and C Squadron with the 2nd South Wales Borderers. Being on the reverse slope, the tanks are protected from enemy observation. In the far background, just visible behind the second tank from the right, the high silhouette of an AVRE- assault bridge can be seen crawling up the incline. (IWM BU 854)

the entire crew became casualties. The second went up on a mine. The three remaining Crabs pressed through and succeeded in reaching the edge of the enemy stronghold. Here the troop leader's tank was hit and burst into flames, killing the entire crew. The last two tanks were ordered back to widen the lane. One blew up

when doing so, but nevertheless a 16-foot lane had been achieved by 1845-hrs.

In the centre (Lane 5), No. 2 Troop, under Lieutenant Hugh Mundy, lost two tanks on mines. The remaining three suffered delays from rotors being jammed by the heavy German wire but

Tank crews of the 7th Royal Tanks observe the pre-assault bombing of the German defence positions by RAF bombers. The forward assault units had been ordered to keep a 2,000-yard safety bomb-line. Picture by Sergeant Wilkes. (IWM BU 855)

they pressed home the assault and had opened a good 30-foot lane by 1900-hrs.

On the left (Lane 6), the team under Sergeant W. Smyth flailed almost straight through to the strongpoint before two tanks fell victim to mines and a third was hit by an AP shell from the enemy gun on the flank. Sergeant Smyth himself turned round to successfully widen the lane, which by 1930-hrs was open for the follow-up armour and troops.

With all three lanes opened by the Crabs, the AVREs of No. 1 Troop, 617th Assault Squadron, went in through them, followed by three troops of Crocodile flame-throwers from A Squadron, 141st RAC; the Churchill gun tanks of C Squadron, 7th Royal Tanks; and the South Wales Borderers infantry, all of them converging on Strongpoint 5.

One AVRE was knocked out by an 88mm, a second went up on a mine, and a third became stuck between a carrier and a derelict tank, leaving three to bombard the concrete pillboxes of the redoubt with their heavy Petard mortars. Meanwhile, the nine Crocodiles drenched the enemy positions in flame. One German platoon, sent in as reinforcements, was caught in the open and completely wiped out by a squirt of flame from a Crocodile.

At 1940-hrs, the 2nd South Wales Borderers attacked with D Company leading, followed by A and B. When D Company crossed the shallow valley it came under shell and small-arms fire from the same wood on the right flank that had troubled the tanks. Among those hit was the company commander, Major Douglas Talmage. However the rest of the company continued to advance across the minefield and, on reaching Strongpoint 5, went over the wire and into the enemy positions. Although the stronghold possessed three anti-tank guns, many mortars and a profusion of Panzerfäuste, the garrison offered almost no opposition. Those Germans remaining in the slit trenches surrendered. The majority – some 40 men – had taken refuge in the large concrete bunker located in the middle of the position and stayed there until the infantry invited them to come out. Within eleven minutes, the strongpoint capitulated.

As A Company under Captain Reed began to pass through to engage the next strongpoint, No. 6, a heavy concentration of German fire fell right in its middle, causing 60 casualties and disorganising the unit, so that only one section reached the objective, too weak to capture it. B Company, assigned to capture strongpoint 7, had its leading platoon pinned down in the open by the same fire. Seeing this, the company commander, Major Donald Collins, led the rest of his men round to the left, through Lane 6, avoiding the enemy fire. They then helped A Company to mop up Strongpoint 6 and, supported by Crocodiles, swept into Strongpoint 7 and cleared it. The anti-tank fire from Strongpoint 8 on the right flank held up any further advance. The AVREs and Crocodiles had to wait an hour before they could move forward to the last objective, finally succeeding in destroying the troublesome 88mm from a flank. By 2240, the South Wales Borderers had taken all their objectives.

Meanwhile, in the centre of 56th Brigade's sector, other gapping teams had launched the assault to open the three lanes of gap 'Hazel', first through the minefield and then across the anti-tank ditch. There was a slight delay owing to the congestion of armoured vehicles in the area. All eight gapping teams for 'Laura', 'Hazel' and 'Mary' had to pass through a bottleneck some 440 yards wide

One of the armoured gapping teams – Flails and AVREs parked in close leaguer whilst hidden from observation by the lie of the land on the Forming-Up Point. This is the team for Lane 7, the right-hand lane of gap 'Hazel'. The mine-flailing Crabs on the left are those of Lieutenant A. Thwaites' No. 2 Troop of C Squadron, 22nd Dragoons. The two AVREs on the right – the 'pilot' tank in front and the bridge-layer behind – are from No. 3 Troop of the 222nd Assault Squadron, RE. Three of Lieutenant Thwaites' five Crabs would be put out of action within ten minutes of H-Hour, but the troop would still complete sweeping its lane through the minefield. However, the assault bridge would be dropped prematurely due to its cable being severed by splinters from mortar fire. A second bridge-layer would go on to rectify the omission and successfully straddle the anti-tank ditch, thus opening up Lane 7. Note the four cows imperturbably grazing the field around the assembled armour! (IWM BU 1195)

between two woods as they moved up from the forming-up point to the start line. The three teams for 'Hazel' started out after the other teams and found many of the guide posts knocked down and tank tracks going off in all directions, which caused them to temporarily lose direction. However, in due course, the three teams reached the start line and began making their breach. The centre lane here (Lane 8) was a hardened road, believed to be free of mines, so Crabs were only used in the two outer lanes.

On the right (Lane 7), No. 2 Troop of C Squadron, led by Lieutenant A. Thwaites, made a bad start, three of its Crabs being out of action

Looking back northwards from the D31 in July 2007.

H-Hour! The armoured gapping teams advance in open formation towards the enemy lines. The copse seen on the far horizon in the centre of the picture is German Strongpoint 5 which was the objective of the three teams of gap 'Laura'. The Flails and AVREs are already way out in front, the Churchills seen in the foreground being those of C Squadron of the 7th Royal Tanks, assigned to go in with the 2nd South Wales Borderers. (IWM BU 1193)

within ten minutes. One went up on a mine, the others had to stop as the blast from successive mines jammed the cutter blades and prevented the drums from revolving. Under mortar fire, the crews stripped the blades and were able to move forward again and by 1915 hrs had cleared their 24-foot lane. The bridge-laying AVRE of the 222nd Assault Squadron moved up but its bridge was hit and fell from its frame. The Snake pulled by the next AVRE was hit and blew up. The reserve bridge was brought up but it too fell prematurely when

still 500 yards from the ditch. The crew had to dismount and winch it up again under heavy mortar fire before successfully placing it over the anti-tank ditch. By 2055 the infantry were crossing in carriers. However, two of the vehicles bogged down in the muddy lane and blocked it until 0330-hrs the next morning.

In the centre (Lane 8), reportedly free of mines, an AVRE bridge-layer of the 222nd Squadron led the breach team, the other AVREs having been held up in the mêlée of tanks in the bottleneck. It ran fast to drop its bridge over the ditch but was stopped dead a few yards from it by an explosion which broke its track. Another AVRE which came up to tow the vehicle off suffered the same fate, as did a scout car, the resultant wreckage leaving the road well and truly blocked. It was later discovered the road was booby trapped with a cache of Teller mines buried deep in the surface and operated remotely by a stick-plunger mechanism connected by wires. Sappers of the divisional 757th Field Company, RE, later swept a track round the knocked-out vehicles, but the road was not cleared, nor the ditch filled by bulldozing until 1500-hrs the following afternoon.

On the left (Lane 9), No. 2 Troop of B Squadron under Sergeant Redmond got two Crabs up to the anti-tank ditch but, as they were completing their turns in heavy ground, mines blew the jib off one and the tracks from the other. The third Crab blew up halfway down the minefield. However, a 20-foot lane was free and up this went the AVRE with its Snake. As the explosive-filled pipe was being pushed over the ditch it struck a mine and blew up with a tremendous blast, wrecking the Crab at the ditch's edge. As it tried to back out, the AVRE hit a mine and blew up. Next, the bridge-laying AVRE (its bridge already damaged by mortar fire) triggered a mine which the Crabs had already safely passed. With so much armour cluttering the path, the lane was abandoned as a failure.

Only one of the three 'Hazel' lanes had been successfully opened but it sufficed. Parts of both assaulting infantry battalions used it when their assigned lanes in 'Laura' and 'Mary' were blocked, as did the supporting armour.

Meanwhile, on the left of the 56th Brigade sector, two troops of B Squadron, 22nd Dragoons, had gone forward to cut open the two lanes of gap 'Mary'.

On the right (Lane 10), No. 3 Troop, commanded by Lieutenant William Shaw and with only four Crabs, suffered complete misfortune. Just past the start line, the leading tank smashed its jib against the bank of a sunken road, putting itself out of action. The second and third tanks, racing up to the minefield, both blew up on mines from a hitherto undiscovered outer minefield. Lieutenant Shaw decided to use his fourth and last tank to open a second entry to Lane 11 on his left but this Crab too went up as it was making its way forward and so Lane 10 remained closed.

On the left (Lane 11), No. 1 Troop under Captain Ian Hammerton met with more success. The troop made a dog-leg route, its elbow lying at the end of the anti-tank ditch. Operating on the extreme left of the assault sector, almost on the edge of a small cliff, the troop flailed for 200 yards without exploding a single mine. By chance, the troop had hit on a gap in the mine-laying. The lead tank broke a track as it reached the forward enemy trenches, but the rest of the troop continued to flail right up to Strongpoint 1. By 1855-hrs the lane had been completed to a width of 24 feet – the first lane open of all eight – and down it went the 2nd Gloucesters infantry in carriers together with two troops of Crocodiles, the six AVREs of No. 3 Troop of the 617th Assault Squadron and the Churchills of B Squadron, 7th Royal Tanks. Two Crocodiles were lost on the start line and another was knocked out in the minefield, leaving just three to flame the enemy trenches with their deadly spurts of fire. One AVRE was immobilised by a mine just off the far end of the lane. Then, as the Churchills began to move through, two of them went a little off the flailed path and both went up on mines in quick succession, blocking the lane for an hour.

Despite these losses, the Gloucesters lost no time in taking their first objectives, Strongpoints 1, 2 and 2a. The AVREs helped by knocking out an 88mm and using its Petard to great effect, dealing with the concrete pillboxes. There was little real resistance. Most German troops surrendered quickly, some of them just waiting in their slit trenches with all their kit packed ready for a journey to the POW cages. At 2035-hrs the Crocodiles flamed Strongpoint No. 3 which quickly became an inferno. Advancing to the next objective, the Crocodiles got off course and missed No. 4, which however fell to the Gloucesters at 2125-hrs, disgorging some 30 prisoners. The Crocodiles then went for Strongpoints 9 and 10 and wiped them out.

Now it was time for the follow-up battalion, the 2nd Essex, to pass through in their Kangaroo armoured personnel carriers, together with their supporting armour, No. 3 Troop of the 617th Assault Squadron and A Squadron of the 7th Royal Tanks. The battalion had orders to drive through whichever gaps were open, going straight for their initial objectives, Strongpoints 9, 9a and 10. By now it was getting dark and in view of the state of the gaps, the heavy going and the failing light, the battalion commander Lieutenant-Colonel Geoffrey Elliott, ordered his troops to dismount from the Kangaroos and take off on foot. He ordered the squadron of tanks to move at once and independently to a rendezvous at Demi-Lieue, just north of Strongpoint 3, where the infantry would catch up.

The Churchills and the by-now dismounted troops of the Essex Regiment used Lane 11 of 'Mary' and Lane 7 of 'Hazel' to pass through the minefield. Although it was now completely dark, both groups found the rendezvous point. At 2330-hrs A Company captured Strongpoints 9 and 9a, and B Company with a troop of tanks (the latter used more for bashing through the tangled trees and undergrowth than for fire support) took Strongpoint 10, netting about 40 prisoners and two female

Smoke rises high from the battle in front as carriers and riflemen of the 2nd South Wales Borderers move forward into the attack on Strongpoint 5. The road crossing the picture from left to right is the D31 from Montivilliers to Fréville.
(IWM BU 1196)

The 49th Division attack was covered by two AFPU photographers, Sergeant Wilkes and Sergeant Max Collins. The two men moved almost side by side, as evidenced by this picture by Collins, taken at the telegraph post that can be seen some 50 yards forward in Wilkes' photo. Note the 'Rommel asparagus' poles, erected as obstacles against airborne landings.
(IWM BU 861)

Another 100 yards or so closer to Strongpoint 5. The South Wales Borderers infantry are moving up behind the Crocodile flame-thrower tanks. The attack through the 'Laura' gap was supported by three troops of Crocodiles from A Squadron of the 141st RAC – Nos. 1, 2 and 3 led by Lieutenant Griggs, Lieutenant Tunbridge and Sergeant Wheatcroft respectively. Three of the nine can be seen in this picture by Sergeant Collins. On the left stands a reserve Flail of the 22nd Dragoons.
(IWM BU 862)

The same view pictured in 2007, looking across the cornfields to the wood that was Strongpoint 5 on the horizon. The line of trees in between marks the line of the D52 road from Montivilliers to Fontaine-la-Mallet.

The attack on Strongpoint 5 in full swing. Riding as a passenger on the deck of one of the Churchill tanks, Sergeant Collins pictured a section of South Wales Borderers moving into the assault behind a Crocodile and stepping aside to make way for Collins' Churchill. They are all in Lane 4 of 'Laura' and are about to cross the Montivilliers to Fontaine-la-Mallet road. Note how the passage of the tanks has churned up the clay soil, softened by recent rain. Up ahead in mid-distance, a little left of centre, the Flails and AVREs of the Lane 5 team can be seen on the slope directly below Strongpoint 5. Further to the right, on the horizon behind Strongpoint 5 lies a second wood – this was the location of Strongpoint 6. (IWM BU 864)

As Collins' tank crosses the road, the slope below Strongpoint 5 comes in full view, just in time for him to catch two of the Crocodiles launching their deadly jets of fire on the enemy trenches. As the report by A Squadron of the 141st RAC put it: 'The Crocs went through the gap with the infantry and absolutely soaked position 5 in flame. It was a magnificent and awe-inspiring sight and the infantry entered immediately afterwards.' On the extreme left (visible as a dark strip) is the stretch of anti-tank ditch to be crossed by the 'Hazel' gapping teams. (IWM BU 865)

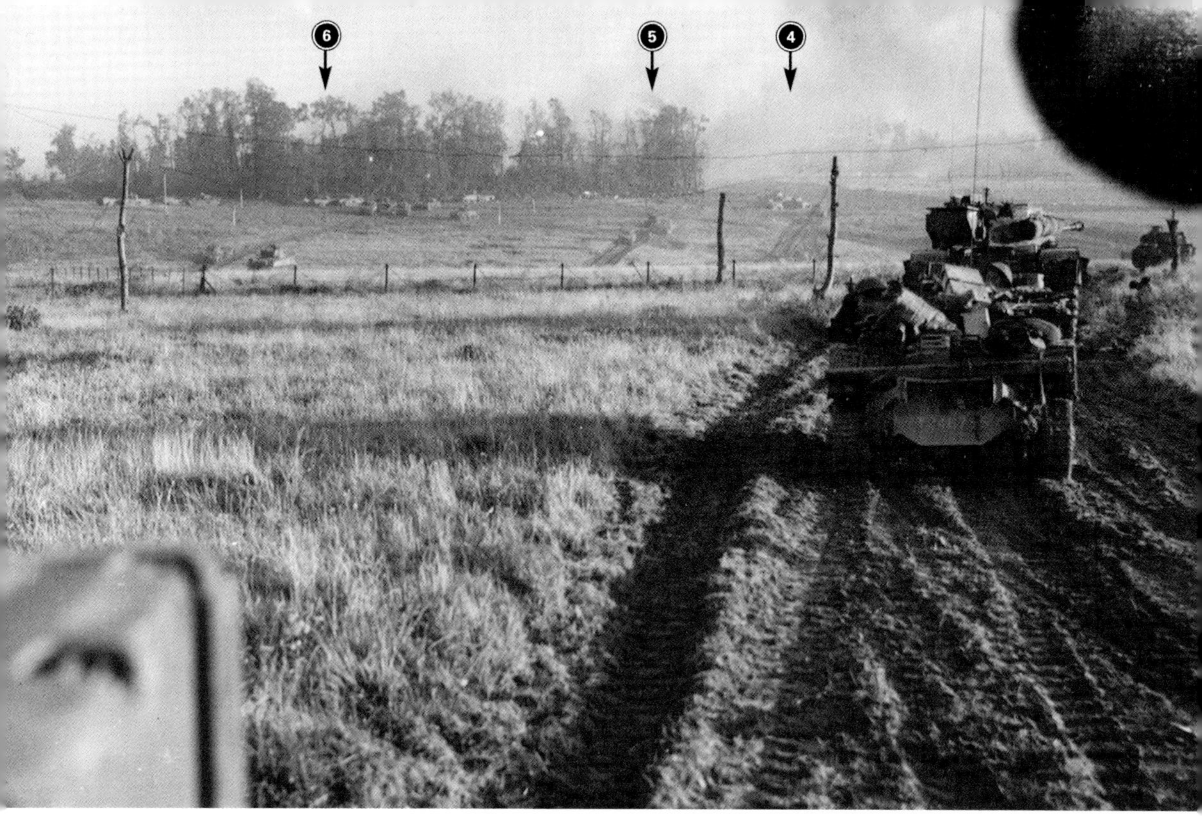
6
5
4

Moving in on the deck of another Churchill a few minutes later, Sergeant Wilkes by pure coincidence took a picture from exactly the same spot, and a sharper one fortunately. All three lanes of gap 'Laura' are plainly visible below Strongpoint 5 –their numbers are marked on the photograph. The edge of the German position is crawling with British tanks: a troop of three Crocodiles can be discerned on the left and four Flails of Sergeant Smyth's troop can be seen at the top of Lane 6; the troop's fifth tank stands lower down, knocked out in the minefield. Two Flails of Lieutenant Mundy's troop can be seen working their way up in Lane 5 and two of Lieutenant Neil's troop are at the top of Lane 4. The German anti-tank fire that knocked out three of the Flails and one AVRE came in from Strongpoint 8, which is out of the picture to the right. Strongpoint 6, beyond 5, is masked in smoke. The carrier in the foreground is a Royal Artillery observation post vehicle with a forward observation officer directing fire. (IWM BU 1191)

Peace and quiet has returned to the northern plateau and the trees that once hid a German stronghold.

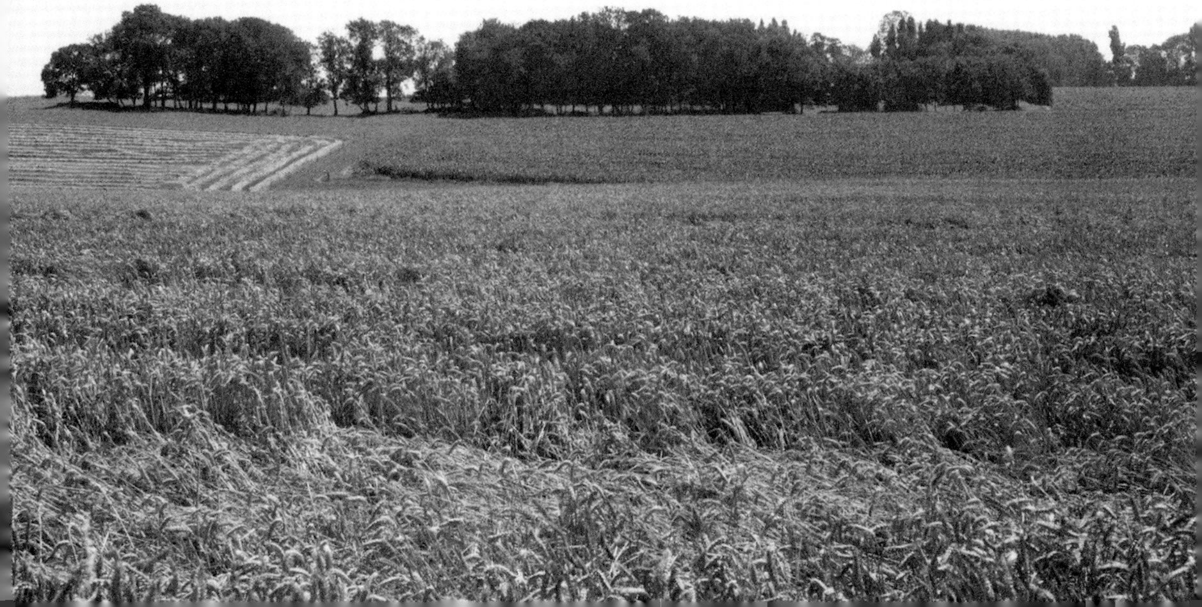

Hidden under the foliage, the German fortifications remain. German Strongpoint 5 actually comprised the grounds of a farm, the Ferme d'Eprémesnil, and several of the concrete structures erected by the Germans survive in situ today. This pillbox (a Regelbau 58c – or 'Tobruk' as the Allies called them) stands on the north-west corner of the farm. We are looking back across the shallow valley where the minefield lay and from where the Allied assault came. The occupants of the pillbox had a clear view of the enemy tanks coming towards them.

Strongpoint 5 fell to D Company of the South Wales Borderers at 1951-hrs but Strongpoint 6, locally known as the Hameau d'Eprémesnil, was not captured by B Company until 2117. This pillbox guarded its north-east corner. This is not a conventional design as the Germans tended to avoid broad embrasures and side openings like this. It may have been an observation post of some kind.

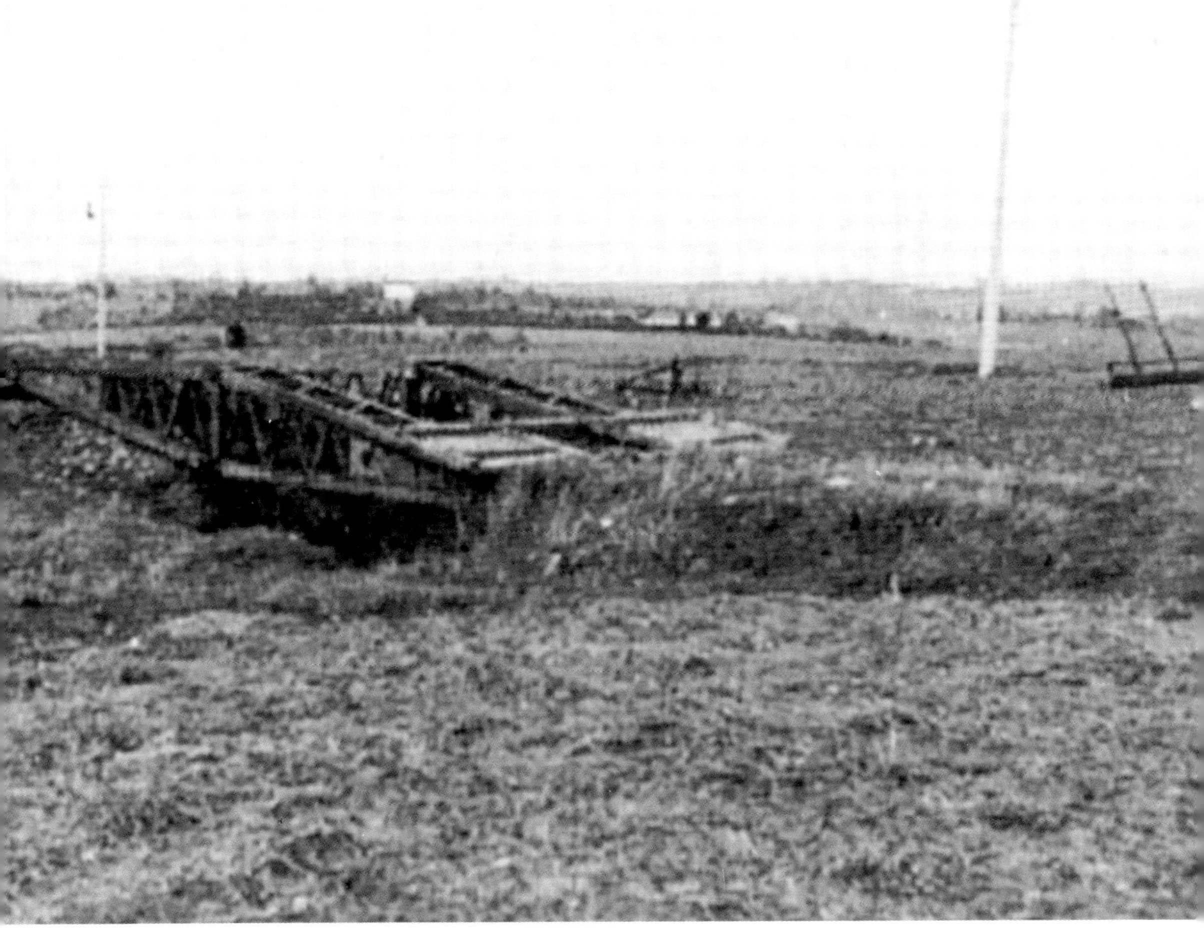

Of the three lanes of gap 'Hazel', only one – Lane 7 – was successfully opened by the gapping teams. This is the AVRE bridge that was put over the anti-tank ditch in this lane by No. 3 Troop of the 222nd Assault Squadron. By the time this picture was taken in 1947 most of the ditch had already been filled in. The line of telegraph poles behind locates the small road that marked the course of Lane 8. Assumed to be free of mines, its gapping team was not preceded by Flails. However, the roadway proved to be infested with deeply-buried Teller mines, which blew up two AVREs and a scout car, effectively blocking the lane.

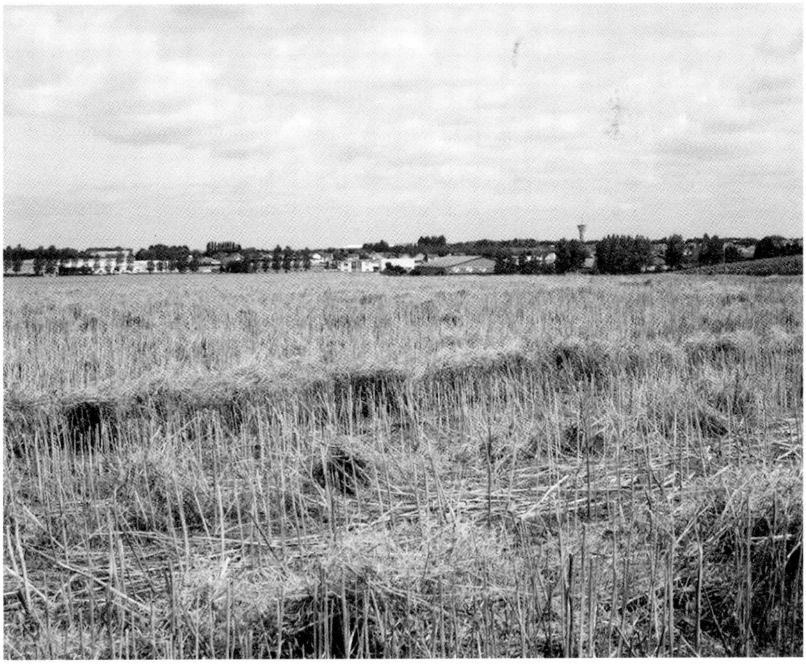

The same view today, looking back to the first houses of Montivilliers. The small road coming up the incline is locally known as the Chemin de Rouelles.

Just before twilight, Sergeant Collins caught an AVRE which, according to the caption, has just fired its Petard mortar, lobbing one of its 40lb 'Flying Dustbins' onto an enemy target. This particular vehicle has elsewhere been suggested to be AVRE 3B of No. 3 Troop of the 617th Assault Squadron – one of those that went up Lane 11. However, the sequence of this frame in Sergeant Collins's series of pictures and the fact that Collins was going in through Lane 4, which was some 600 yards away from Lane 11, make that conclusion rather unlikely. (IWM BU 863)

camp followers. The Essex did not really have to fight for the objectives, the Crocodiles having practically taken the positions for them.

Both companies then cleared the south end of the northern plateau and A Company seized two intact bridges over the Fontaine river at La Bouteillerie. It was now too late to launch an attack across the river and on to the escarpment of the southern plateau, so Colonel Elliott ordered his men to stand fast.

Meanwhile, the supporting AVREs were not idle. To the left of where 56th Brigade was operating, divisional sappers (756th Field Company, RE and No. 3 Platoon, 240th Field Company, RE) were trying to clear the main road and a track running south-west from Montivilliers to Le Havre for the 147th Brigade and in particular that part short of Strongpoint 9, which was heavily mined and blocked. Major John Alexander, commanding 617th Squadron, came to their aid by leading five AVREs of his HQ and No. 2 Troops down from the plateau – on foot, in darkness, down a 40-degree slope sown with 'S' mines – to the main road. They located the road-block which was found to consist of two concrete walls four feet thick with a crater in between. The AVREs demolished the barricade with 200lbs of explosive, then cleared a second to allow a bulldozer to fill in the crater. The 'dozer went up on a mine but the job was finished by 0700-hrs in the morning.

The remaining three AVREs of No. 2 Troop made two additional crossings over the Fontaine river – under fire – using fascines and chespale towed to the site in armoured sledges. Another AVRE struggled all night to bring an SBG bridge 6,000 yards through darkness only to drop it off on two unforeseen humps 100 yards short of the stream. Fortunately it was not needed.

51st DIVISION (Phase I)

At midnight, six and a quarter hours after the 49th Division had gone into the assault, the 51st Division joined the attack, launching its 152nd Brigade (Brigadier Jim Cassel) with an objective of capturing Strongpoint 8 and securing a base in the area north of the Forêt de Montgeon.

As with the 56th Brigade on its immediate left, the brigade's assault began with armoured gapping teams opening up lanes across the anti-tank ditch and through the minefield on the far side. The special armour assigned to the brigade for this purpose were the Flails of B Squadron of the 1st Lothians and Border Yeomanry and three troops of AVREs from the 16th and 284th Assault Squadrons, with Sherman tanks of the East Riding Yeomanry in support.

A German 8.8cm PaK 43/41 anti-tank gun of Strongpoint 3, photographed some time after the battle. Built around another farm, the Ferme de la Coudraie, Strongpoint 3 was flamed by the Crocodiles and captured by the 2nd Gloucesters at 2035-hrs. The view is eastward, looking across the valley of the Lézarde to the high ground beyond.

The 22nd Dragoons lost no less than 29 of their 35 Flail tanks employed in opening up breaches 'Laura', 'Hazel' and 'Mary' for the 49th Division. Most of those lost in the attack were subsequently recovered but this particular tank still remained in situ in 1947, bogged down in the field where it had been disabled by a mine three years earlier.

Three lanes had been planned, about 50 yards apart and code-named 'Gin', 'Rum' and 'Ale'. However, it had been agreed that the 49th Division would make one of its breaches – 'Laura' – available to the 51st Division by H plus 5 hours (2245-hrs), i.e. 75 minutes before the division's own gapping teams were to go in. This would enable the 152nd Brigade's lead battalion, the 5th Seaforths, to assault Strongpoint 8 ahead of the special armour.

It was now well into the night. To help the gapping teams find their way in the darkness, three special aids had been planned. Firstly, 'artificial moonlight' – searchlights reflecting their beams on clouds – would begin lighting up the battlefield as soon as it got dark. Secondly, the routes of the three gapping teams from their start line to the edge of the anti-tank ditch – a distance of some 1,000 yards – would be marked as far forward as possible by green lights hung on the German anti-airlanding posts that dotted the fields. Thirdly, a Bofors gun firing four tracer rounds over the middle lane every two minutes would give further direction.

However, as is often the case with set-piece attacks, things did not work out quite as planned. Firstly, the night was cloudless, so the searchlights did not reflect much light onto the ground. Then, as the teams set off, it was found that many posts with the guiding lanterns had been knocked down by vehicles that had passed earlier. Worse, unknown to the tank commanders, the Bofors gun was off line, firing at a tangent some 200 yards too far to the right. The result was that all three gapping teams had difficulty finding their assigned crossing points. Also, due to heavy going, they took nearly twice as long – 100 instead of 50 minutes – to reach the ditch.

On the left, the team for gap 'Ale' (Lane 3) – AVREs of No. 3 Troop, 16th Assault Squadron, and Flails of No. 1 Troop, Lothians and Border, under command of Major Ronald Watson – found that the left-hand directional lights were not there and, following the Bofors, reached the ditch about where the centre lane should have been. The team's Snake had been broken during a change of direction, so the AVREs 'petarded' the far bank in order to attempt to detonate any mines; the bridge-layer then put down its bridge; and the four Flails under Lieutenant Peter Carter crossed over and successfully cleared a path about 200 yards long without encountering any mines. However, as the troop headed for the squadron rallying point, one Flail blew up on a mine as did Major Watson's HQ Troop Sherman when it tried to take cover from a German anti-tank gun. Later that night the remaining three tanks tried to widen the breach down the hillside, which they succeeded in doing, but all three blew up on mines doing so, two of them while reversing back up an already swept lane.

In the centre, the team for 'Rum' (Lane 2) – AVREs of No. 2 Troop, 16th Squadron, and Flails of No. 2 Troop, Lothians, under command of Major John Willott – was equally unfortunate. As he reached the last lights about 500 yards from the ditch, the Lane Commander in the lead AVRE was put in a quandary when he noted that the direction of the Bofors and the lights on the ground did not correspond. Deciding that the Bofors was likely the more reliable guidance, he swung his column to the right. Luckily he soon spotted a large house which he knew to be at the extreme edge of the ditch, realised his error, and swung left again, reaching the ditch where the right-hand lane should have been. The team blew its Snake (accidentally blowing flat the members of the neighbouring 'Gin' team, who had not received the radioed warning), the bridge was laid down, the run-up to it was filled with small fascines, and the Flails under Lieutenant William Boreham crossed over. The lead one cleared a path up to the road but then stuck on a tree stump and bellied. The second Flail caught some steel piping in its rotor which jammed and put it out of the running. The next two blew up on mines, but the fifth and last one carried on, joining its lane with that of the 'Gin' team coming in from the right.

As a result of the misdirected manoeuvre of the centre team, the team for 'Gin' (Lane 1) on the right – AVREs of No. 1 Troop, 284th Squadron, and Flails of No. 4 Troop, Lothians, under command of Major John Blomfield – had to turn to make way and, when they turned back, came to the ditch which stymied their manoeuvre. Although now at right angles to their planned course, the AVREs blew their Snake (in their turn blowing the members of 'Rum' team flat), put down the bridge and fascines, and the Flails under Lieutenant David Melville crossed over and successfully swept a path down to the track leading to Fontaine-la-Mallet, as they were supposed to do. However, all five tanks were blown up in the process.

Thus, by 0300-hrs, two lanes were by no means through the minefield yet and one was blocked by three Flails. Sappers of the 275th Field Company, RE, were ordered forward to improve the gaps, which they did, despite being under fire. By 0400 'Rum' was fit for personnel on foot and thirty-five minutes later for vehicles.

Meanwhile, at 2315-hrs, the 5th Seaforths, lead battalion of the 152nd Brigade, had detoured into the 49th Division's sector and passed through 'Laura' gap as planned. Despite being heavily shelled and the men having to manhandle their equipment down into the anti-tank ditch and up the other side, they went forward and captured Strongpoint 8.

The 5th Camerons followed next and, moving through the 'Ale' gap at 0410-hrs under heavy shelling and turning west, took Strongpoint 11. Picking up a telephone found in a concrete post there,

The attack by the 51st (Highland) Division began at midnight but no pictures exist of the night-time operations to open its breaches 'Gin', 'Rum' and 'Ale'. However, Sergeant Collins photographed one of the division's armoured gapping teams in the forming-up area during the afternoon preceding the attack. The four Flails are from B Squadron of the Lothians and Border Yeomanry and the AVREs in the field behind (the second one a bridge-layer) are either from the 16th or from the 284th Assault Squadron, RE. The unit to which the infantrymen belonged is unidentified but may be the 5th Seaforth Highlanders. (IWM BU 859)

Major Alfred Parker of D Company got through to the German garrison command in Le Havre and promptly invited them to surrender – to which the German on the other end refused, 'with a hollow laugh'. By first light, the two battalions were firmly dug in the ruins of at Fontaine-la-Mallet, which had been devastated by the aerial bombardment.

Meanwhile, the operation was developing so successfully that Major-General Tom Rennie, the 51st Division commander, decided

In the last couple of decades Montivilliers has expanded over much of the forming-up area. This is the view looking north-east from the D52 at the point where Lane 3 ('Ale') once crossed it.

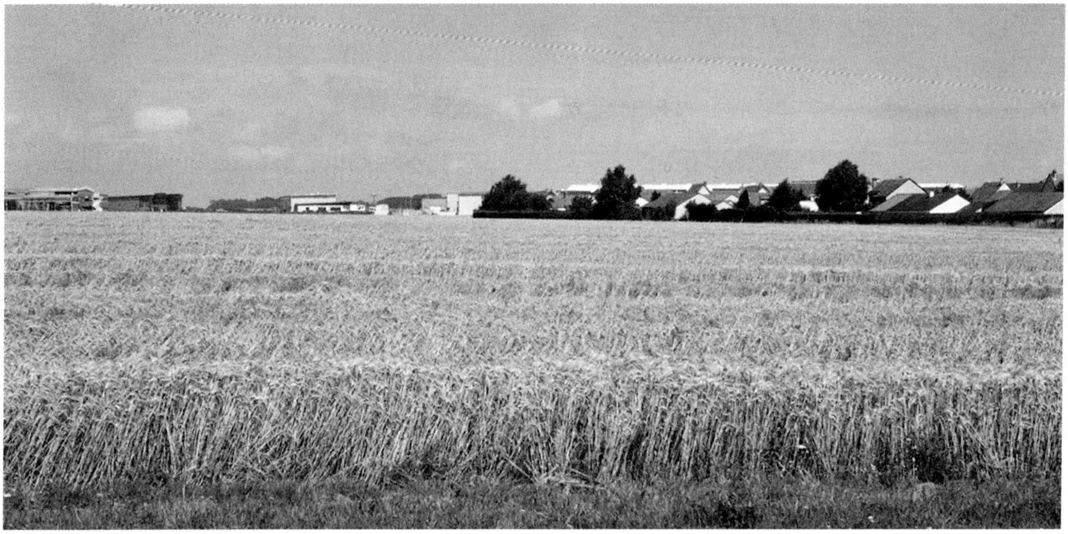

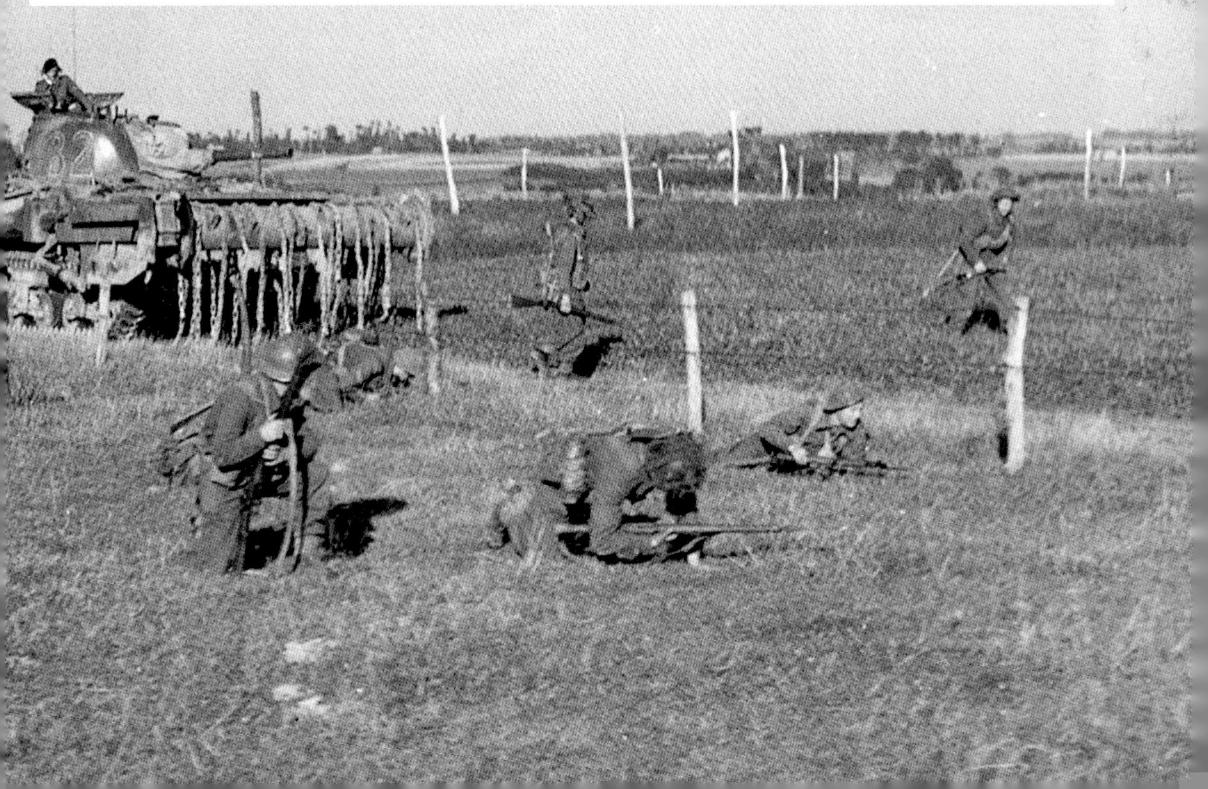

to push the start of Phase III forward and pass through the lead unit of the exploiting 153rd Brigade (Brigadier Nap Murray). At 0425, the 1st Gordons crossed the minefield through 'Rum' and, crossing the Fontaine river, reached the edge of the Forêt de Montgeon by 1100, where they repulsed an attempted counter-attack. Due to the many wrecked vehicles in the minefield lanes, the battalion's supporting

The bridge dropped over the anti-tank ditch by No. 2 Troop of the 16th Assault Squadron in Lane 2 ('Rum'). The gapping team for this lane had been misguided by the directional fire from the Bofors, which was firing at an angle from the intended line, and put down its bridge where Lane 1 ('Gin') should have been.

Although the ditch has long been filled in, the manor house in the background, the Manoir de la Frévillière, allowed Karel Margry to pin-point the exact spot where the bridge lay (even if he had to sneak into the garden to get his comparison). The house stands just north of the D52.

B Squadron of the Lothians and Border Yeomanry lost its entire strength – 15 Crabs – whilst mine-sweeping the three lanes for the 51st Division. Twelve of the Flails blew up on Teller mines (one was in addition hit by an German anti-tank shell which hit the engine compartment), two fell out due to technical failures and one bellied on a tree stump. The squadron personnel and the regimental REME Light Aid Detachment spent all of 12th September recovering the disabled tanks from the assault area. Here two Sherman Armoured Recovery Vehicles pull one of the Crabs from the field where it was stopped.

Flails, Crocodiles, AVREs and Shermans were unable to follow and so were delayed in reaching the forward position. By this point congestion in the serviceable gaps was acute. Two of the three assault bridges had become dislodged and sappers were trying to put another across.

The 2nd Seaforths of 152nd Brigade, following behind the Gordons, had also had to leave their supporting armour on the wrong side of the obstacle but by first light were advancing on Les Monts-Trottins.

By 0800-hrs on the morning of 11th September, both the 49th and 51st Divisions had successfully breached the enemy defences north of Le Havre and captured all of their initial objectives, including 11 strongpoints on the northern plateau and two bridges over the Fontaine. The success of the operation owed much to the efforts of the armoured gapping teams, but these had paid a heavy price, not so much in personnel but in matériel. Of the total force of 35 Crabs and six Shermans employed by the 22nd Dragoons in the assault, no fewer than 29 Crabs and three Shermans had been lost or seriously damaged in the minefields. The Lothians and Border Yeomanry had suffered even worse, all 15 of their Crabs and one HQ Troop Sherman being put out of action. The 222nd and 617th Assault Squadrons had lost six AVREs, the 141st RAC three Crocodiles and the 7th Royal Tanks four Churchills. In all, some 60 armoured vehicles littered the fields east of Fontaine-la-Mallet that morning.

11th SEPTEMBER

49th DIVISION (Phase II)

Early on the morning of 11th September, Bomber Command made its final attack on Le Havre, 171 aircraft (out of 218 despatched) dropping 864 tons of bombs on two targets in the western part of the town. Visibility was good, but the Master Bomber ordered the final wave to cease bombing because of smoke and dust.

On the German side, command during the hours of darkness was almost impossible with all means of communication, wireless and roads hopelessly damaged. Companies thrown in as reserves reached their assembly points late, and with numerous casualties. When daylight came, Oberst Wildermuth realised a counter-attack was out of the question and ordered his troops to take up defensive positions in the second line, on the east and north-east edge of the Forêt de Montgeon.

Meanwhile, in 49th Division's sector, the 147th Brigade (Brigadier Henry Wood) had begun operations planned for Phase II. The brigade was to advance on the left of 56th Brigade, from Montivilliers south-westwards, through the defile west of the Lézarde river, then across the river with the intention of capturing the southern plateau.

When the sappers started to sweep the road and track south-west from Montivilliers it was immediately discovered that both were heavily mined. It was therefore decided that the 1st Leicesters should proceed without supporting tanks or vehicles while the sappers concentrated on getting the route through Demi-Lieue open. The Leicesters were lucky enough to meet a stray troop of Churchills from the 7th Royal Tanks and took them under their wing. The group reached their objective, the bridge over the Fontaine at La Bouteillerie, by 0915-hrs. On their arrival they found that it had already been secured by the 2nd Essex during the night.

Next, the 11th Royal Scots Fusiliers pushed across the river and established a good bridgehead on the southern plateau. At 1300-hrs they proceeded to carry out the mission originally allotted to the 7th Duke of Wellington Regiment to clear the whole plateau. The task proved harder than expected, owing to the number of strongpoints and fortified houses to be taken. The 617th Assault Squadron had been put in support of 147th Brigade and, having crossed the river, joined the battalion. Their AVREs assisted two company attacks during the afternoon, but the Royal Scots Fusiliers would not complete the capture of the plateau until the following day.

Meanwhile, the 7th Duke of Wellington Regiment moved down from Montivilliers in Kangaroos. Relieved of their task to clear the

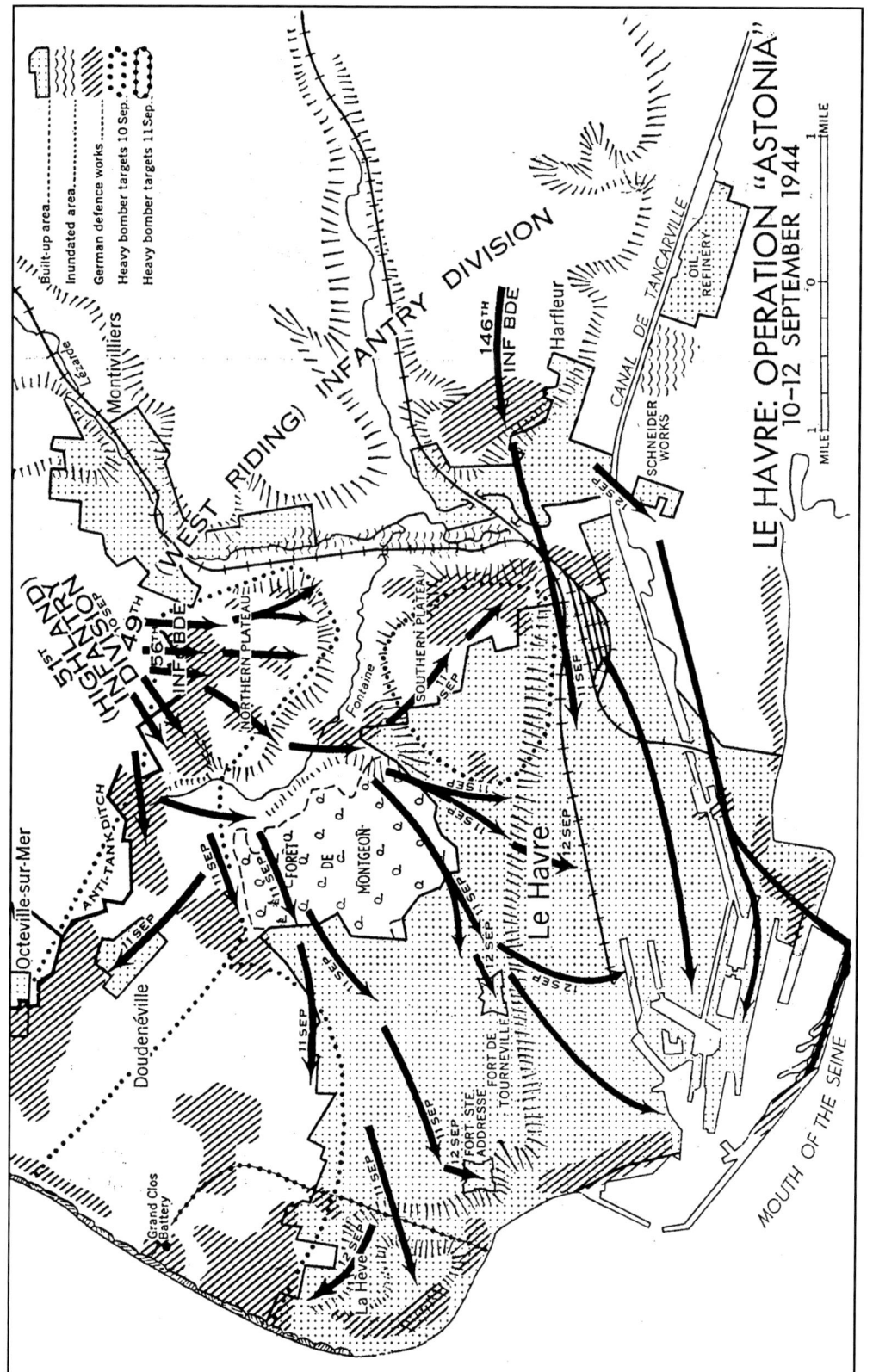

Once the break-in was achieved, the 49th and 51st Divisions advanced towards Le Havre largely as had been planned. Early on 11th September, the 146th Brigade joined the fray, attacking from the east through Harfleur.

Operation 'Astonia' • 47

southern plateau, the plan was now that they should advance straight into Le Havre. However, the road was still not completely clear of obstacles, as discovered when two of the Kangaroos ran over mines. The convoy was halted and the troops ordered to dismount at the bridge held by the Leicesters.

On hearing this, the commander of the Gloucesters, Lieutenant-Colonel Francis Butterworth, asked for permission to push on. His battalion was in position near the bridge captured by the 2nd Essex a little further west. Permission was readily granted. C Company took the lead, mounted on the Churchill tanks of B Squadron, 7th Royal Tanks. They passed east of the Forêt de Montgeon and entered Le Havre, reaching the Place de la Liberté, an aptly-named square in the north-east (upper) section of the town. Civilians began to appear, as did large numbers of Free French resistance members, who proved most useful in getting prisoners to the rear.

The advance was resumed in the early evening, this time with D Company mounted on the tanks. As they approached the Fort de Tourneville the lead Churchill was fired on by an anti-tank gun from the fort. While the tanks returned fire, a platoon made a right flanking move allowing Sergeant Maclean, with three shots from a PIAT, to damage the gun sufficiently to stop it firing. By now dusk was approaching, and the battalion halted for the night. They dug in close by the adjacent Sainte-Marie Cemetery with the intention of tackling the fort on the morrow.

49th DIVISION (Phase III)

On the morning of 11th September, as 147th Brigade was pushing down into Le Havre from the north-east, the 146th Brigade joined the attack. They were situated east of the Lézarde river and were beginning the operation planned for Phase III, the capture of Harfleur. This would then allow them to advance into Le Havre from the east. Barring the way into Harfleur were two enemy strongholds, both sited in orchards south of the main road and about 400 yards apart. The one on the right, bordering on the road, had been given the code-name 'Oscar' and the one on the left was 'Oswald'. The objective of taking them had been given to the 1/4th King's Own Yorkshire Light Infantry. In support were the Churchill tanks of A Squadron, 9th Royal Tanks; two troops of flail tanks from C Squadron, 22nd Dragoons; one troop of Crocodiles from A Squadron, 141st RAC; and the AVREs of No. 2 Troop, 222nd Assault Squadron.

It had been decided to attack before dawn, so as to prevent enemy observation from the high ground across the Lézarde, but this meant the infantry would have to go in without flails or close-support fire from the tanks. It proved an unhappy choice. B Company's assault on 'Oswald' at 0530-hrs was broken up with severe losses from heavy machine-gun fire and C Company's attack on 'Oscar' at 0545-hrs got stuck in the minefields. The commanding officer, Lieutenant-Colonel Thomas Harrison-Topham decided to pull back and renew the attack after daylight with use of the Flails, tanks and Crocodiles.

After three Crabs of No. 4 Troop had cleared a gap in the minefield right up to 'Oscar' (two of them bogging down in the process), C Company went in at 0930-hrs and captured the position, taking 57 prisoners. The German commander of 'Oswald' then asked for an hour's truce to evacuate the wounded and bury the dead, but Brigadier John Walker refused this and instead gave him until noon to surrender. The German officer said he could not do this without permission and so the attack went in at 1230-hrs. The Crabs made two gaps, blowing about 50 mines (two of the flails going up on mines); the Crocodiles went in spurting their jets of flame, and the objective was captured by 1335-hrs, its dugouts disgorging another 72 prisoners who came running out of the wood with their hands up.

Progress was then rapid. At 1400-hrs, the 4th Lincolns passed through to advance into Harfleur along two routes. A Company with two AVREs, an armoured bulldozer and divisional sappers of 294th Field Company proceeded down the main road, which was blocked by road-blocks at four points. The AVREs demolished these with Wade charges and Petard projectiles. The dozer then cleared away the debris and filled in craters, whilst the sappers checked the road and verges for mines. Thus the main road was made passable for wheeled vehicles.

Meanwhile the rest of the 4th Lincolns with other AVREs proceeded down a more southerly route, moving cross-country and down a lane south of 'Oswald'. Considering the potential strength of the enemy defences, opposition was comparatively light. The Lincolns suffered 14 casualties, mainly from enemy machine guns firing from concrete emplacements in Harfleur, but these were quickly subdued by the AVREs with their Petards. The AVREs also dealt with an anti-tank ditch encountered on the forward slope, filling it by blowing down trees. Entering Harfleur, the Lincolns found the bridges there intact, giving them a bridgehead over the Lézarde. Advancing from this and along the line of the Canal Vauban, the battalion was established on the outskirts of Le Havre by nightfall.

Before dawn a German medical officer, who had been running a hospital in another part of the Jenner Tunnel, now in no man's land, sent a French Red Cross orderly to contact the British as he wished

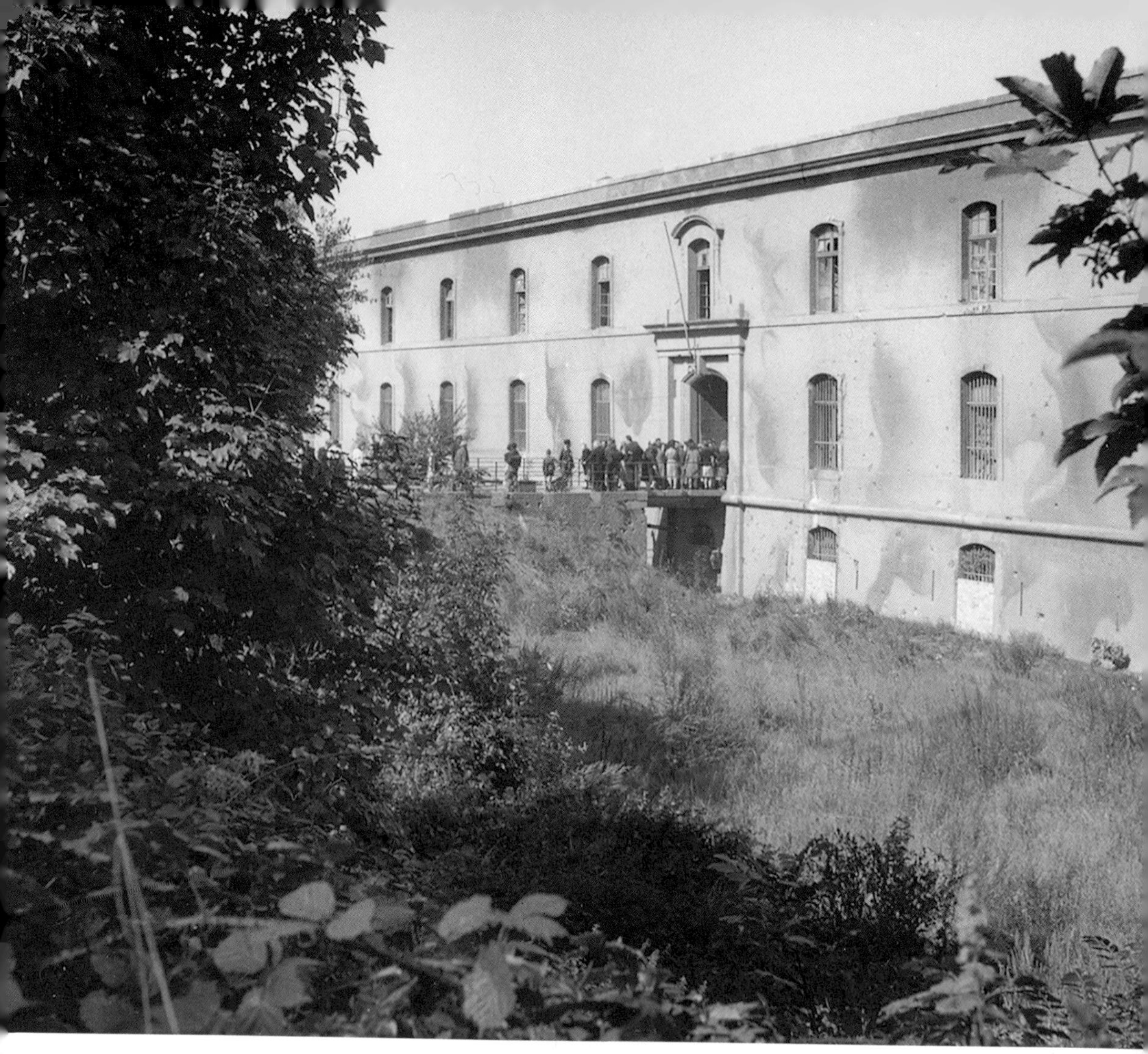

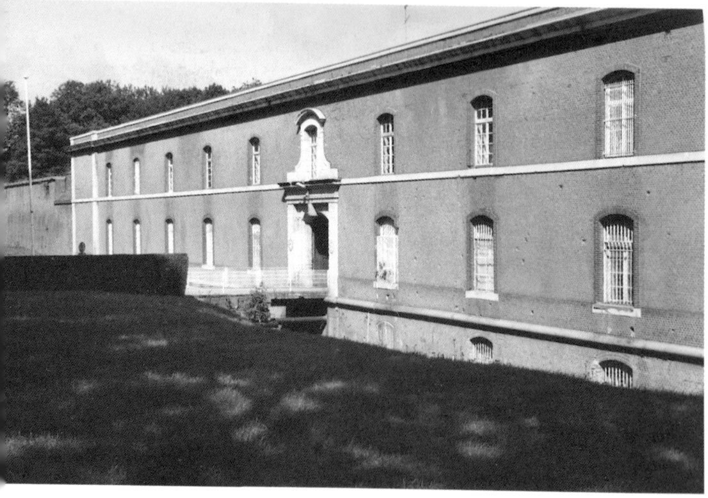

The French Army used the fort until 1976. By the turn of the millennium it housed the Municipal Archives and is today a community arts centre.

The first British troops penetrated into Le Havre in the late afternoon of 11th September, both the 49th and the 51st Divisions entering parts of the Ville Haute. Coming in from the north-east and advancing down the Rue du 329ème Régiment d'Infanterie, in the early evening the 2nd Gloucesters and supporting tanks from B Squadron of the 7th Royal Tanks came up against the Fort de Tourneville. Erected between 1854 and 1860, as one of the forts to protect Le Havre after the medieval city ramparts had been pulled down, and a French Army regimental barracks since 1890, its sturdy walls and moat presented a daunting obstacle. The Germans had turned it into a strongpoint and Oberst Wildermuth moved his command post there late on the 11th. It promised to be a tough nut to crack but, to the surprise and relief of the British, the garrison surrendered without resistance at 1100 on the 12th after a 20-minute barrage by tanks and mortars. (IWM BU 904)

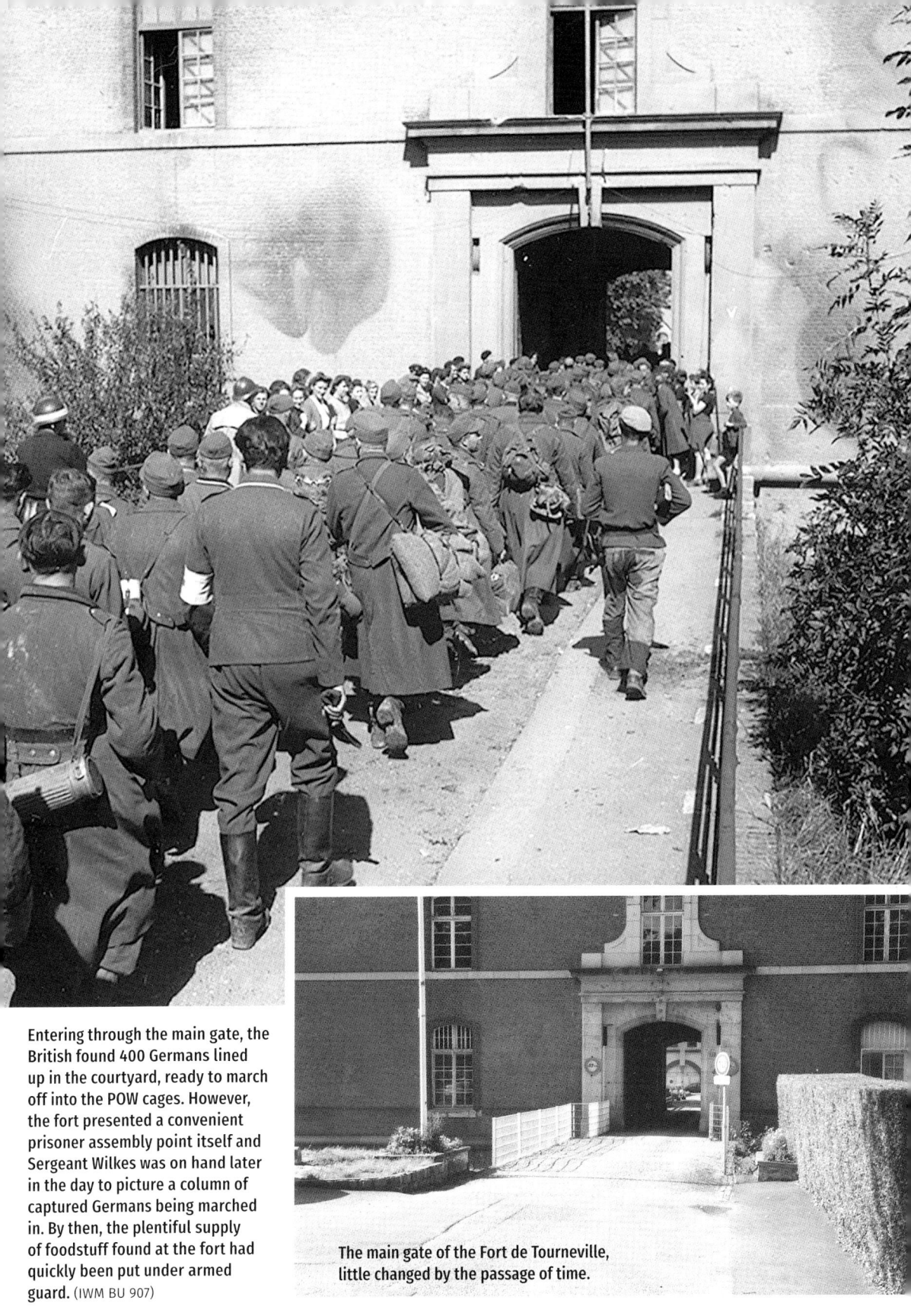

Entering through the main gate, the British found 400 Germans lined up in the courtyard, ready to march off into the POW cages. However, the fort presented a convenient prisoner assembly point itself and Sergeant Wilkes was on hand later in the day to picture a column of captured Germans being marched in. By then, the plentiful supply of foodstuff found at the fort had quickly been put under armed guard. (IWM BU 907)

The main gate of the Fort de Tourneville, little changed by the passage of time.

to surrender himself and his staff and patients. The French emissary contacted the 2nd Gloucesters. Captain Herbert Lovett accompanied the orderly back to the tunnel and found around 200 wounded German casualties with attendant orderlies.

51st DIVISION (Phase III)

As the 49th Division secured a foothold in the northern and eastern outskirts of Le Havre on 11th September, the 51st Division had been busy to the north-west. By mid-morning, the division's supporting tank detachments had finally been able to make their passage through the minefields and around noon they joined up with their assigned infantry units.

In 152nd Brigade's sector, the Shermans of B Squadron of the East Riding Yeomanry paired up with the 2nd Seaforths outside Fontaine-la-Mallet and immediately went for the enemy strongpoint at Hill 67 at Les Monts-Trottins. A short shelling from 2,000 yards sufficed for the Germans to raise a white flag. Moving on to Dondenéville the force was met by hundreds of Germans, completely demoralised by the tremendous non-stop air and artillery bombardment and with no fight left in them.

Further south, the 1st Gordons of 153rd Brigade, dug in on the northern edge of the Forêt de Montgeon. There they were joined by the brigade's supporting armour at 1230-hrs – Flails of C Squadron, Lothians; Crocodiles of C Squadron, 141st RAC; AVREs of 284th Assault Squadron; and the Shermans of the 144th RAC. The combined force immediately moved down two roads through the forest to engage the two German gun positions at Févretot and Ste Catherine. At Févretot the more northerly of the two was engaged by the Gordons' A Company. The Flails had hardly commenced clearing a lane into it when white flags were waived over the German gun positions and some 100 Germans surrendered. The southern stronghold, attacked by C Company, proved equally acquiescent and both positions were taken by 1600-hrs.

The brigade's two other battalions, the 5th Black Watch and the 5/7th Gordons, then passed through the forest and in the early evening penetrated into the north-western quarters of the upper part of the city against negligible resistance. The only obstruction they encountered was from the exuberant French population cheering their liberators and from flocks of disconsolate Germans trying to surrender.

The Highland Division's third brigade, the 154th (Brigadier James Oliver), deployed only one battalion, the 7th Black Watch.

It was not until the early hours of the 12th that the first British troops descended into the lower part of the city. Here a Churchill of the 7th Royal Tanks, with 49th Division infantry mounted on its deck, rolls across the Place Thiers on its way to the Hôtel de Ville. They are on the edge of the inner-city area laid to waste by the RAF bombardment of 5th September.
(JEAN PAUL DUBOSQ)

The same spot today, looking across the square into what was in 1944 the Rue de Montivilliers and is today named the Rue d'Ingouville.

Supported by Shermans of the Northamptonshire Yeomanry, they began moving through the minefields in Kangaroos at 1400-hrs. They advanced slowly through the demolished suburbs of Le Havre, before heading to Cap de la Hève to the north-west of the town to capture the Naval Barracks there. The tanks were held up by craters, so the infantry went forward alone. They attacked the barracks but in this instance the Germans were more minded to put up some resistance. Unable to force a conclusion, the British dug in for the night.

Meanwhile 'Grayforce' started out for the German military aerodrome at Octeville-sur-Mer further to the north-west. This battlegroup was made up of the tanks of A Squadron of the Northamptonshire Yeomanry under command of Major Gray Skelton, accompanied by an infantry section of the Derbyshire Yeomanry in half-tracks.

12th SEPTEMBER

By the morning of 12th September, the German situation was clearly hopeless. British infantry and armour were closing in on the city centre and the Allied artillery fire continued remorselessly. Communications had broken down completely and there were hardly any anti-tank guns left. The stage was now set for the final act.

The 51st Division completed the cleaning-out of the enemy positions outside the city proper. At 0900-hrs 'Grayforce' arrived at the Octeville aerodrome and, sweeping round it they reached the coast. There they found white flags waving over the coastal guns and bunkers of the Atlantic Wall. As the force's tanks deployed, a column of three officers and 357 men of Kriegsmarine Artillery streamed out to surrender.

The 2nd Seaforths of 152nd Brigade captured another 1,000 prisoners at the enemy coastal battery and strongpoint at Octeville. Much of this was due to Captain Henri Salman, commander of B Squadron, East Riding Yeomanry. Salman was a Belgian national who before the war had been a novitiate, intent on joining the clergy. He spoke fluent German. Dismounted, his revolver in hand, he led two of his tank troops in front of the infantry, yelling at the Germans to come out, which they did in droves.

Further south, the 7th Black Watch of 154th Brigade completed cleaning out the enemy positions at Cap de la Hève, their supporting tanks shooting up whatever pillbox or obstacle they encountered.

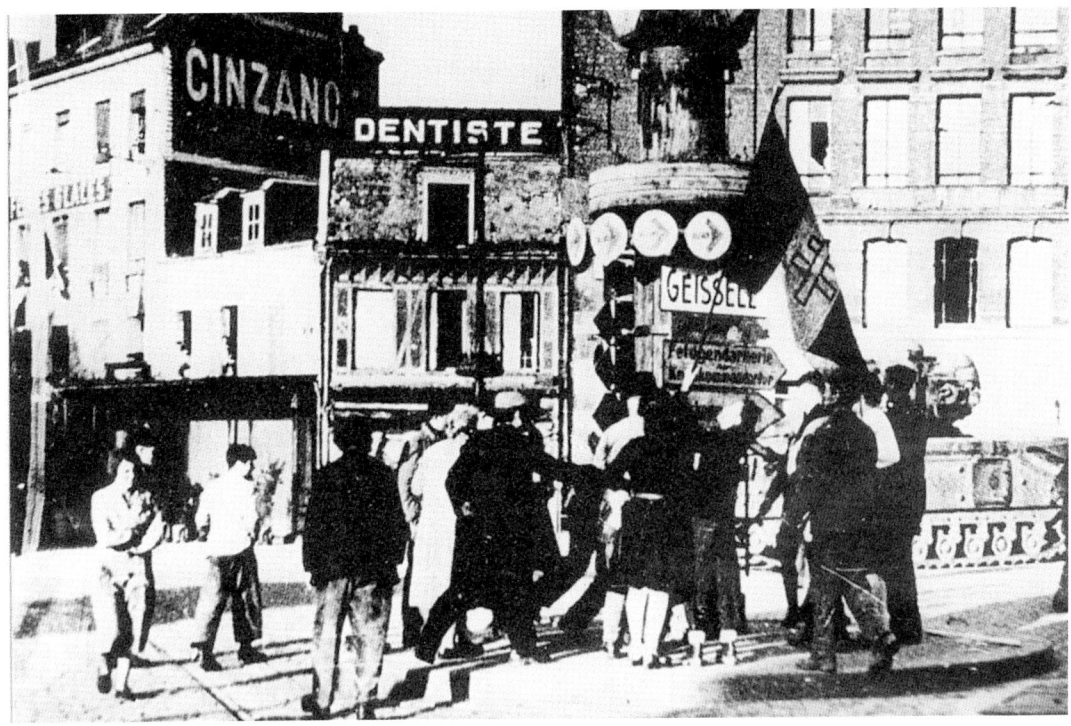

As soon as the liberators had arrived (note the Churchill in the background), the citizens of Le Havre came out on the streets with Croix de Lorraine flags and fell upon the German traffic signs, pulling down these hated symbols of Nazi occupation, like here on the Rond-Point, the main crossroads at the north-eastern corner of the Ville Bas. Scenes like these occurred in all liberated towns of France but at Le Havre the acts of joy were decidedly more subdued owing to the sadness and mourning prevailing after the massive destruction and loss of life caused by the air raids of the previous week. (JEAN CLAUDE PIGNY)

This corner of Le Havre was relatively unaffected by the bombing and all buildings visible in this image from 2007 remain as they were. However, the Quatre Cadrans (Four Dials) clock pylon which stood on the corner has since disappeared.

By 1100-hrs they had collected 1,100 prisoners. The other two battalions of the brigade, the 1st Black Watch and the 7th Argylls, were not required to take part in the attack.

Meanwhile, the 153rd Brigade had entered the north-western part of Le Havre proper. As the 5/7th Gordons, riding on the tanks of C Squadron, 144th RAC, approached the Fort de Ste Adresse, the enemy detonated remote-controlled mines. Expecting a heavy battle for the fort, two troops of Crocodiles from C Squadron, 141st RAC, were called forward. The Crocodiles, Shermans and the Gordons infantry were all primed for action, ready to attack, when at 1530-hrs the garrison hoisted a white flag and surrendered. Seven officers and 242 other ranks were taken prisoner.

However, the greater part of Le Havre was to be the responsibility of 49th Division. That morning, in the eastern part of the city, the 146th Brigade had been preparing its further advance. The road bridges over both the railway and river were found to be very badly damaged by the Allied bombing and German demolitions The brigade had hoped to use these bridges for its move forward but that proved impossible. An alternative route was finally found on the low ground between the main road and the Canal de Tancarville.

At 0800-hrs, the brigade's attack into the city began. The 4th Lincolns accompanied by B Squadron, 9th Royal Tanks, advanced on the right and the Hallamshire battalion, with C Squadron and two AVREs, on the left. They were moving into the lower part of Le Havre – a built-up area consisting of high blocks of workers flats, warehouses, docks and repair shops – and the routes of both battalions were completely overlooked by the escarpment to their right. An enemy gun opened up on the Hallams from the height but an urgent request to 147th Brigade, responsible for that area, soon led to it being silenced. The Lincolns encountered a number of enemy strongpoints, housing an anti-tank gun and numerous machine-gun nests, but these were soon overcome. Progress was slow due to the roads being pock-marked with bomb craters and the piled rubble from ruined buildings which blocked their passage. However, by mid-morning the brigade had passed the big Schneider motor works (dismantled by the Germans during the war), seized German strongholds at the telephone exchange and brewery, and begun clearing the docks and marshalling yards. As the Hallams crossed the canal bridge into the Bassin Bellot docks, there was a series of enormous explosions close by. German engineers had blown up the nearby sluice gates. As a precaution

'Troops of the Gloucestershire Regiment enter the town', says the caption of this picture by Sergeant Wilkes. (IWM BU 901)

It was taken in Rue des Gobelins, indeed not far from the city centre, though the troops are actually not entering but leaving. They are moving back up to the Ville Haute, to the north of the city, after completing the clearance of the area of the beachfront on the western side of town. The photograph was taken facing north-east, towards the Place Alphonse Martin.

Operation 'Astonia' • 57

A little further up the road, the same troops pass an FFI resistance fighter and a group of civilians listening to a broadcast beside a British loudspeaker van. The people carrying valises and other luggage have just emerged from one of the tunnels in the escarpment rock where they had found refuge from the bombs and shelling during the past week. (IWM BU 902)

The street at this point is named Rue Georges Lafaurie and the church is the Chapelle St-Michel d'Ingouville.

Lieutenant-Colonel Trevor Hart Dyke, commanding the Hallams, temporarily pulled his troops back.

Meanwhile, further west and in 56th Brigade's sector, the Gloucesters and the 7th Royal Tanks prepared to attack the Fort de Tourneville. As was becoming the norm, their preparation proved unnecessary. After the Churchills and heavy mortars had bombarded the stronghold, a white flag was seen being hoisted over the fort. Cautiously, an infantry platoon made their way inside. There they found the German garrison of some 400 troops lined up in the courtyard, with baggage already packed, waiting to be led away. Among the prisoners was Oberst Erwin von Steinhardt, the Artillerie-Führer (chief artillery commander) of Le Havre. Within the fort they also came across four captured RAF airmen, along with 30 Algerians, 30 Italians and some French women.

Shortly after, at 1115-hrs, a tank troop of B Squadron, 7th Royal Tanks, captured the German garrison commander, Oberst Wildermuth, at his HQ bunker in the nearby Rue Félix Faure. Wildermuth had been wounded in the thigh and stomach by shrapnel a few hours before and therefore surrendered from his bed – in his pyjamas but wearing his medals. His surrender was received by Lieutenant Kit Bland, the troop commander. Wildermuth, his orderly and staff were sent riding upon the top of a Stuart light tank back to 49th Divisional Headquarters, which had by then been set up in the Place de la Liberté. There Wildermuth formally surrendered the city to General Barber.

With the removal of the German command, resistance gradually ceased and white flags began to appear all over the city. However, sporadic fighting continued and a few isolated posts attempted to hold out – though these were soon overcome.

During the afternoon, the battalions of the 56th Brigade continued their advance into the city, each having been given a designated sector to clear. The Gloucesters marched straight through the bomb-shattered centre of Le Havre to the seafront, large numbers of Germans surrendering to them as they did so. In all, the battalion took 1,827 prisoners, among them Konteradmiral Hans-Udo von Tresckow, the See-Kommandant Seine-Somme (naval commander Seine-Somme). He had been holed up in his bunker in the harbour and completely out of touch with the battle, so had sent a British prisoner of war to contact the British. Lieutenant-Colonel Butterworth of the Gloucesters immediately drove down to accept the admiral's surrender.

The 2nd South Wales Borderers, having moved forward with their supporting tanks (C Squadron, 7th Royal Tanks) into the outskirts

Among those captured at the Fort de Tourneville was Oberst Erwin von Steinhardt, the commander of Heeres-Küsten-Artillerie-Regiment 1254 (which manned the Army coastal batteries in Le Havre), who combined this post with that of Artillerie-Führer (Chief Artillery Commander) of the garrison. He is seen here (second left) with his captor, Major Stewart Howard-Jones, the CO of B Squadron of the 7th Royal Tanks, who is holding the colonel's dagger. Sergeant Wilkes' caption identifies the other German officers as (L-R) Oberst Ludwig, Oberst Kynzoriz and Hauptmann Jakob Heberle. (IWM BU 903)

of Le Havre the previous evening and having spent the night near the Sainte-Marie Cemetery, moved down into the city centre and the seaward docks. Not much resistance was met. D Company came under fire from a 20mm gun and a machine gun, but Company Sergeant Major Cude managed to chase off the crews of both with a Bren-gun.

The 2nd Essex, with their supporting tanks, reached the burned-out shell of the Hôtel de Ville in the bomb-blasted heart of the city. Acting on information from an FFI major that the municipal jail in the Rue Lesueur was full of Gestapo and collaborators, they advanced on the

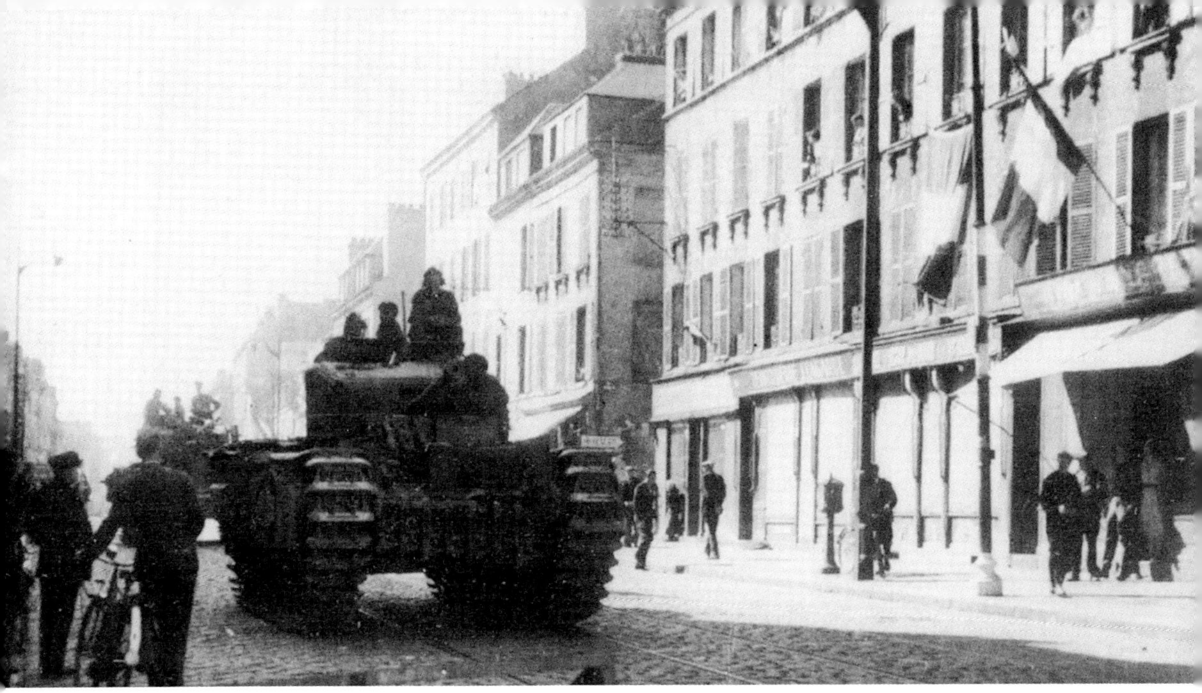

Churchills of the 7th Royal Tanks driving down the Rue Aristide Briand in the afternoon of 12th September. Most armoured units employed in Operation 'Astonia' left Le Havre immediately after completion of the fighting, the specialised armour of the 79th Armoured Division being urgently needed at Boulogne for Operation 'Wellhit' and the 33rd Armoured and 34th Tank Brigades moving to rest areas outside Le Havre, both being stranded like the 49th and 51st Divisions as their transport was needed to ferry supplies to the distant front line in Belgium. (M. LECESNE)

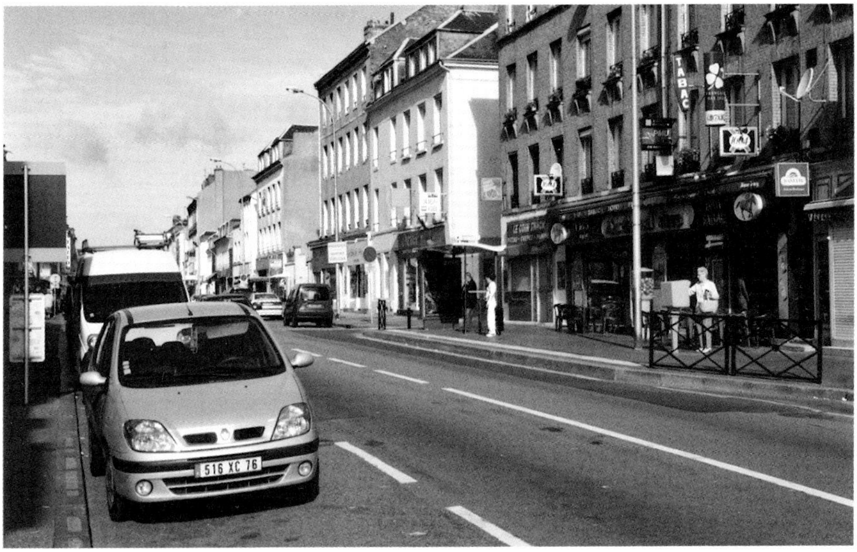
TABAC
516 XC 76

Rue Aristide Briand is the main thoroughfare leading into Le Havre from the east. The picture was taken from just beyond the corner of Rue Berthelot, looking west towards the city centre. The house on the right is No. 263.

prison and, after clearing away the many FFI fighters that were milling around armed to the teeth with captured weapons, surrounded the building. A Churchill tank then blasted down the gates and the Essex infantry entered, only to find all the Germans and their Quislings gone. The battalion ended the day near the Bassin Vauban.

In 147th Brigade's sector, the 11th Royal Scots Fusiliers completed the capture of the southern plateau, overcoming several strongpoints

Oberst Wildermuth, the German Festungskommandant, had not been found at the fort. He had been wounded during the morning and moved to a nearby command post bunker where he was discovered and taken prisoner at 1115-hrs. He and Oberst von Steinhardt and the other captured senior officers were immediately despatched by Stuart light tank to the Place de la Liberté in Le Havre-Aplemont, where Major-General Evelyn Barber of the 49th Division had by then set up his headquarters and where Wildermuth officially capitulated to the British at 1215-hrs. Here, von Steinhardt (standing left, in long coat) and the other German officers await the end of the proceedings. The tank is a 'sawn-off-Stuart', the turret having been removed to lower its silhouette.

Looking west from the Place de la Liberté into the Avenue Rouget de l'Isle on another sunny day in July 2007.

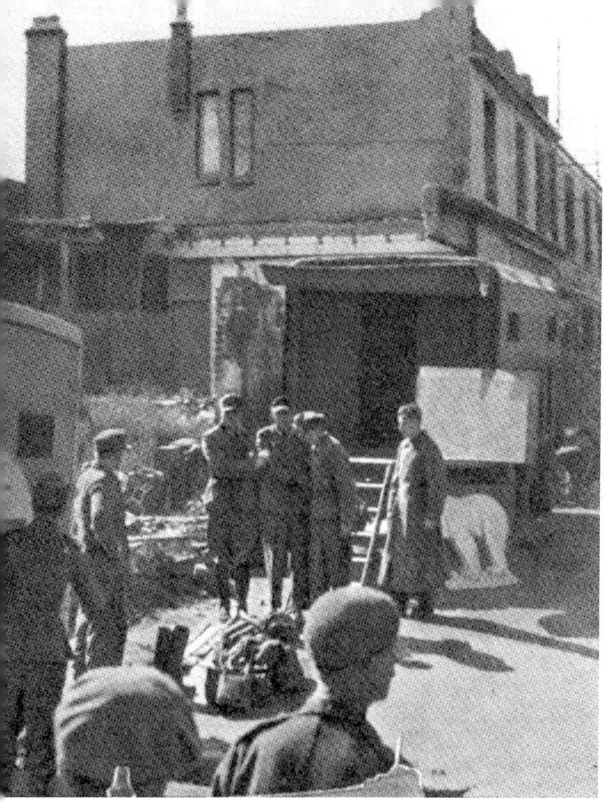

The formal surrender over, Oberst Wildermuth is being helped to an ambulance that will take him to a British field hospital in order to get his thigh and stomach wounds treated.

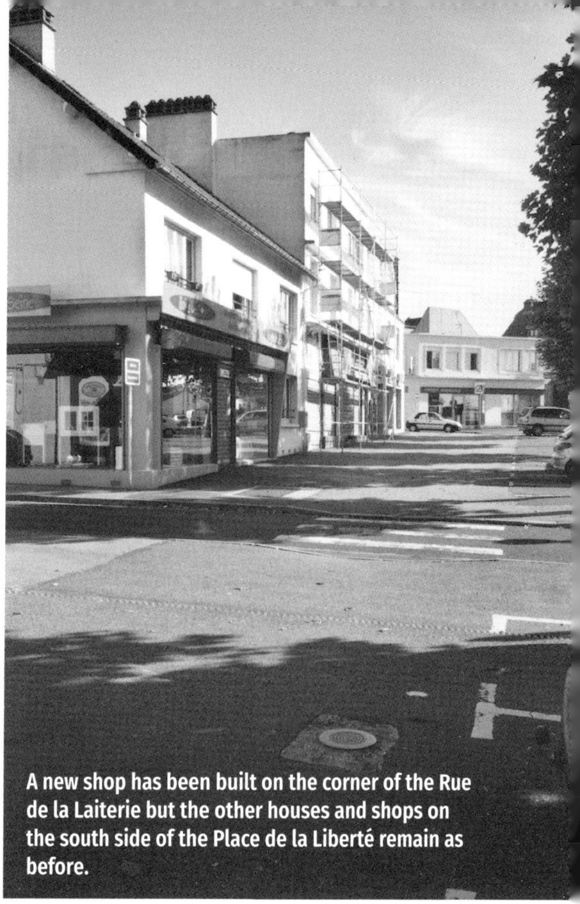

A new shop has been built on the corner of the Rue de la Laiterie but the other houses and shops on the south side of the Place de la Liberté remain as before.

Standing on the platform of his command post caravan, General Barber (right) and one of his staff officers, Major Thomas Coate (left), see Wildermuth off.

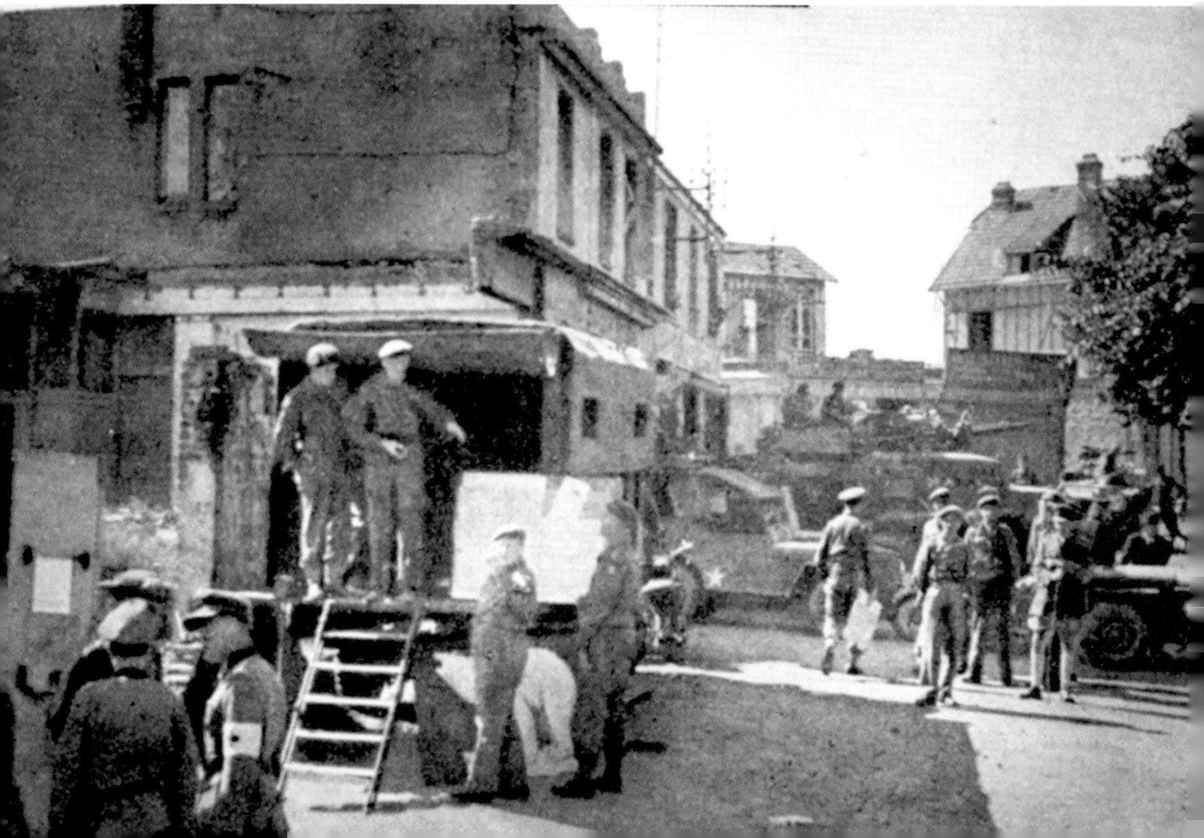

and taking some 300 prisoners. A supporting AVRE of the 617th Squadron was hit by an 88mm and blew up, its entire crew being killed. The 7th Duke of Wellingtons, pulled out of the battle the previous day, crossed the Fontaine bridge and helped clear a built-up part in the south-western corner of the plateau, occupying the escarpment overlooking the Seine estuary.

A thorough search of the eastern docks was made in 146th Brigade's sector by the 4th Lincolns and the Hallamshire battalion, the Lincolns rounding up over 500 prisoners, and the Hallams taking another 1,000 plus taking possession of three Dornier flying-boats and a submarine. By early evening, all of the docks had been cleared except the harbour's South Mole, which extended into the sea for one mile and was studded with casemates and pillboxes. Lieutenant-Colonel Hart Dyke of the Hallams personally led a platoon of his men across the wooden railway bridge that gave access to the mole and cautiously approached the bunkers. Fortunately they proved to be undefended. On their foray, they accepted the surrender of another 80 Germans. It was the last act. By 2200-hrs that evening, all of Le Havre had fallen.

The corps commander, Lieutenant-General Sir John Crocker, visited the 49th Division Headquarters to congratulate General Barber on the German capitulation. He was presented with the pistol which Lieutenant Kit Bland had taken off Wildermuth at his capture. Here Crocker is talking with some staff officers.

The same view photographed 63 years after the event, looking east from the square into the Rue des Hallattes.

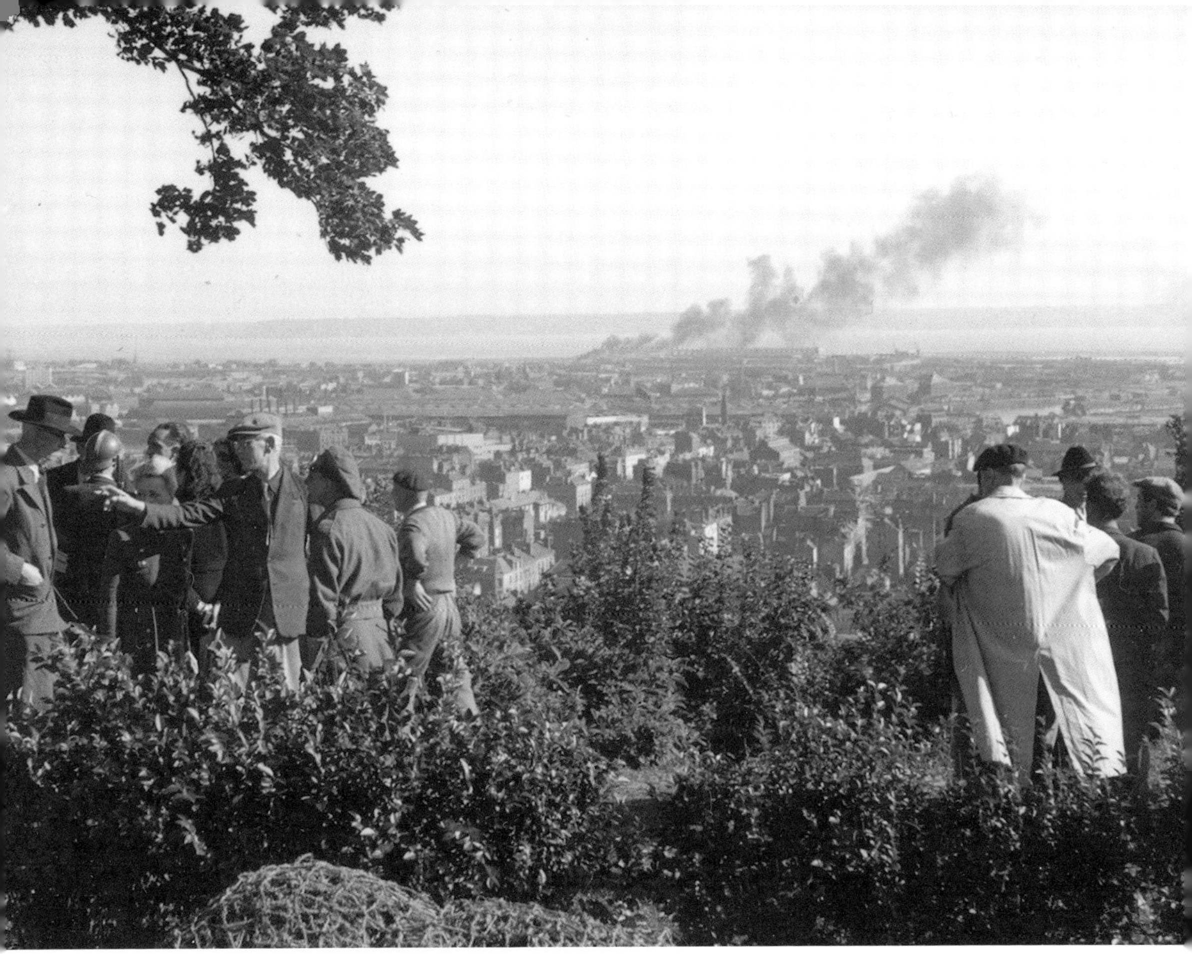

The capture of Le Havre was a classic example of a successful set-piece battle. After the German defences had been 'softened up' by colossal aerial and naval bombardment plus artillery shelling, a 'siege-train' of specialised armour broke through the outer crust of the German defensive perimeter and allowed two British infantry divisions to push through the gap and methodically reduce the enemy strongholds before driving into the heart of the city. Here, in the late afternoon of 12th September, British soldiers, French FFI resistance fighters and other Le Havre citizens watch British shells falling on the last German strongholds in the dock area, pictured by British Army photographer Sergeant Albert Wilkes. (IWM BU 917)

The picture taken by Sergeant Wilkes shows the edge of the escarpment that constitutes the upper part of Le Havre and overlooks the lower town – chiefly comprising the docks and the city centre. More precisely, the men are standing among the bushes close to the Terrasse Amiral Mouchez, opposite the Rue André Messager.

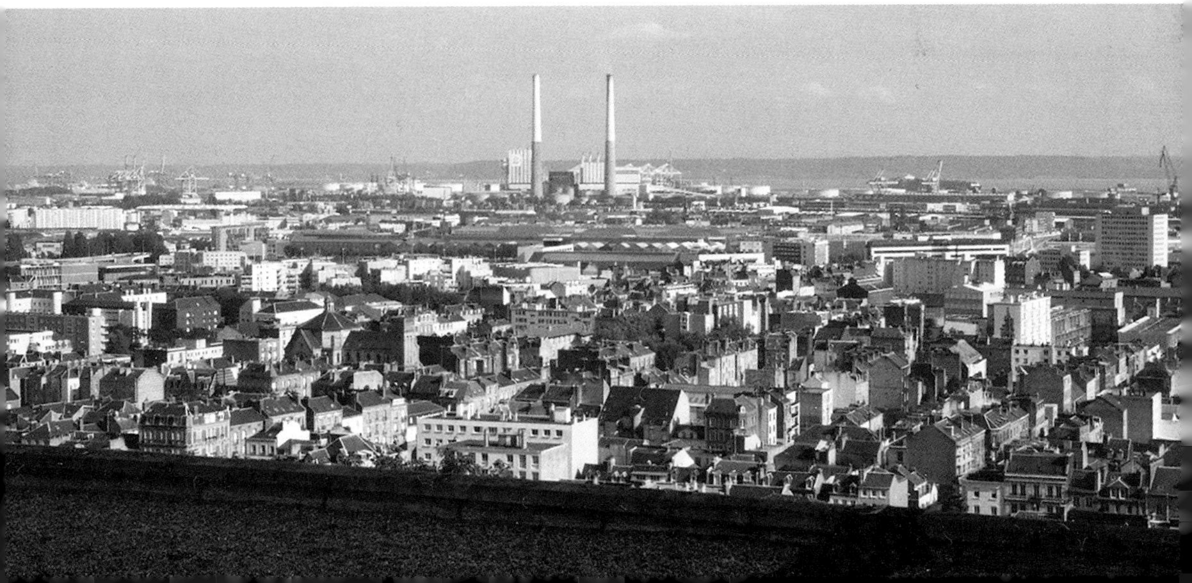

AS THE DUST SETTLES

Despite being strongly fortified and with sufficient supplies for it to have held out for weeks, the formidable Festung Le Havre had yielded within 48 hours. It was the most successful of any of the siege-assaults on the ports of France. Over 11,000 prisoners had been bagged at a cost of less than 500 British casualties. The whole of the 49th Division had suffered only 62 men killed, three missing and 208 wounded, the 51st Division had 35 killed and 103 wounded, and the supporting armoured units 16 men killed and 32 wounded.

The total number of German prisoners came to 11,302 – of which the 49th Division was responsible for 6,900 and the 51st Division brought up the remaining 4,400. An estimated 600 German soldiers had been killed. Vast quantities of stores, guns and vehicles fell into British hands. Many of the German strongholds, particularly the two forts, were found to be very well stocked with wine, spirits and liquors

Some of the 11,300 German prisoners being marched off under guard. All of the British units deployed in Operation 'Astonia' recorded the capture of hundreds of enemy troops, the biggest haul falling to the 2nd Gloucesters who reported having taken 1,827 prisoners. (IWM BU 908)

Sergeant Wilkes pictured the POWs on the Rue du 329ème Régiment d'Infanterie. The head of the column has just passed the Fort de Tourneville, which is off to the right.

Wilkes identified these two female POWs as 'collaborators', which would imply they were French, but they could equally have been German nationals serving as auxiliaries.
(IWM BU 906)

Three FFI men – one a policeman, the other two members of the Equipes Nationales (the Vichy-French voluntary auxiliary youth organisation) – have guided a Humber scout car of the 141st RAC to the Rue Félix Faure in the upper town to seek out German snipers and hideouts. Located just west of the Fort de Tourneville, this street housed several German headquarters during the occupation and it was in a bunker on the corner of Rue Félix Faure and Rue Begouen, a little over 100 metres in the background of this image, that Oberst Wildermuth was taken prisoner. (IWM BU 916)

The house on the right was No. 48 in 1944 but today it is No. 294.

as well as butter, cheese, tinned fruit and other produce. The stores were quickly put under guard and a limited distribution of luxuries was made to the units that had taken part in the assault.

Most observers agreed that the speedy success of Operation 'Astonia' was due to a number of factors: first, careful planning based on full and accurate information of the enemy's positions; second, the bombardment of the enemy defences by the Royal Air Force, Royal Navy and Royal Artillery; third, the success of the initial breaches by the Flails and AVREs; and fourth, the energy with which all troops taking part had exploited the breakthrough.

Perhaps equally importantly, however, the success was attributable to the refusal of the defenders to play the part demanded of them by Berlin. The potential strength of the German defences was enormous and, resolutely defended, their redoubts should have held out much longer than they did. The Germans had offered a respectable but not a fanatical defence. The main reason for this was the position taken by Oberst Wildermuth. Seeing the hopelessness of his situation, Wildermuth was not prepared to sacrifice the lives of his men in a futile Wagnerian struggle to the last. As early as 9th September, he

Operation 'Astonia' • 69

Universal carriers ascending the Rue Clément Marical in the north-west part of the city centre. The caption that goes with Sergeant Wilkes' photo says they belonged to the 2nd Gloucesters. However, the tactical Arm-of-Service marking on the leading vehicle appears to start with a '4', where the Glocesters' AoS would be 56. Given the GS caps of the crew, it may be that the lead carrier was part of a separate unit. (IWM BU 912)

The cobblestones and tramlines have been lifted, but the building on the right remains.

Sergeant Wilkes probably got the unit identification from these Tommies refreshing themselves at the municipal water pump, which stood at the crossroads seen in the previous picture at the Rue de Sainte-Adresse. The battle over, the men of the 49th Infantry Division were allowed one night to enjoy the cafés and bars of Le Havre, and the wine and spirits seized from the Germans, but were then ordered to areas north of the city to rest and refit. The 51st Division stayed in Le Havre for two weeks, being employed on garrison duties. Both divisions were effectively stranded, their RASC transport being taken away from them to help supply other units of British Second Army fighting in northern Belgium. (IWM BU 911)

The water pump has gone but the Aux 4 Chemins shop remained in 2007. Today the building remains, though the shop is deserted. It is the same building seen in the picture top, right of the opposite page.

Operation 'Astonia' • 71

A Frenchman surveys the devastation caused by the bombing. This is the Rue Pierre Faure, looking south from the Rue des Gobelins. (IWM BU 909)

It took many years of reconstruction but Le Havre has risen from the ashes. Only the wall on the left remains as a link with the past.

had given orders to all his officers that 'Allied infantry attacks were to be opposed everywhere, even with side arms only' – but that 'in the event of attacks by tanks, resistance nests which no longer had any anti-tank weapons were then at liberty to surrender'. This explains why so many of the German strongholds raised white flags as soon as tanks appeared on the scene.

Interrogations of German prisoners produced some interesting reactions to the weapons and methods employed by their adversary. The mine-clearing Flail tanks came as a complete novelty to them – they thought it 'sheer madness' when they heard tanks entering the minefields. The flame-throwing Crocodiles were condemned as 'unfair' and 'un-British'. The artificial moonlight used on the first night created considerable surprise as well, despite the weather conditions limiting its effectiveness.

The British soldiers who entered Le Havre were dismayed by the destruction caused by the bombing. In street after street nothing remained but piles of smoking rubble. The civilians they met were still dazed by the terrible ordeal they had gone through. The whole town was in mourning and there was little of the jubilation experienced in other liberated towns of France. The destruction that befell their city deeply shocked the population and later stories began to circulate that the British had deliberately levelled the port so that it would not compete with Southampton after the war. As one Frenchman said bitterly: 'Nous sommes libérés mais nous n'avons plus de maisons.'

OPERATION 'WELLHIT'
Boulogne

The port looking north-west. This is a picture from a Naval Intelligence Division publication which described Boulogne as 'the premier French fishing port', and 'third in order as a passenger port with trans-Atlantic as well as cross-Channel connections'.

AFTER THE FALL of Le Havre, the next objective for General 'Harry' Crerar's Canadian First Army was to be the capture of Boulogne and clearing the coastal belt with its V-Weapon sites and the cross-Channel gun batteries. This phase of the operation was turned over to Canadian II Corps with the lead role to be played by Canadian 3rd Division. As before the support of the specialised armour of 79th Armoured Division would be key to the operation.

A significant additional imperative for this action stemmed from the presence of the German cross-Channel gun batteries and, more latterly, the V-Weapon sites situated in the Pas-de-Calais region. 21st Army Group was under pressure from those living across the Channel in the south of England who had endured four years of shelling and rocket attacks. Now, they felt that if there was an opportunity to stop these attacks, then it should be taken without further delay.

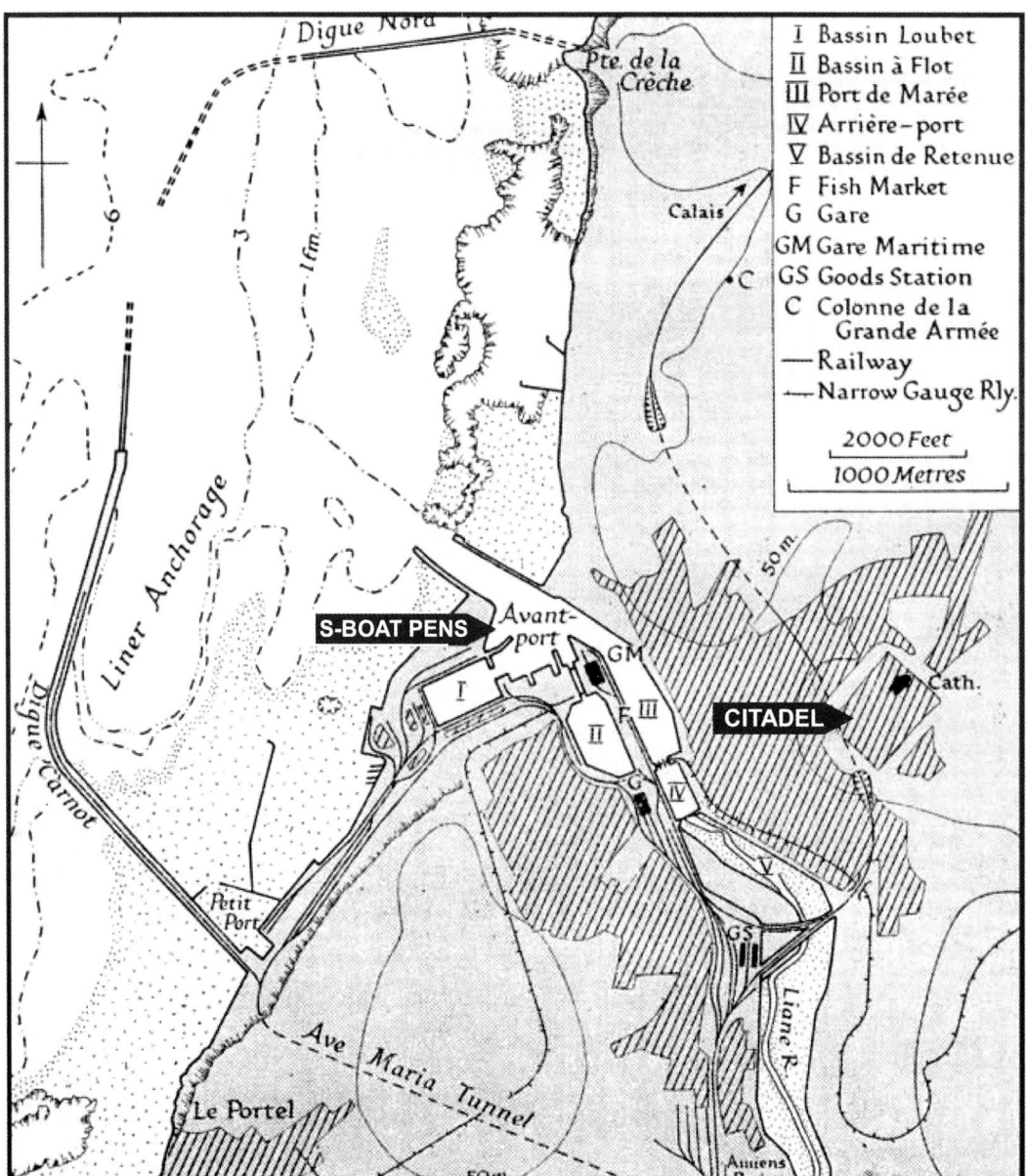

With the commencement of the breakout from the Normandy bridgehead on 25th July, the problem of keeping the rapidly-moving armies properly supplied increased. The loss of the prefabricated Mulberry 'A' at Vierville in the storm in mid-June meant that the vast majority of the resupply of 21st Army Group depended on Mulberry 'B' at Arromanches until a conventional port could be captured. When Cherbourg fell on 29th June, the officer charged with its reconstruction reported that 'the demolition of the port is a masterful job, beyond a doubt the most complete, intensive, and best-planned demolition in history', and it would be many months before it could handle cargo in any quantity. Dieppe and St Valery-en-Caux were entered at the beginning of September but they were tiny by comparison with the deep-water ports of Antwerp, captured on 4th September, and Le Havre, which fell on 12th September. However, the latter could not be brought into operation until mid-October and, although the Antwerp docks were undamaged, they were inland and the Germans still had control of the mouth of the Scheldt. On 5th September, the newly-promoted Field-Marshal Montgomery, commanding 21st Army Group wrote to General Henry Crerar, commanding the Canadian First Army, which had been tasked with capturing the Channel ports, telling him that 'I need Boulogne badly', and asking how soon it could be captured.

Operation 'Wellhit' • 75

At the mouth of the River Liane lies the French coastal port of Boulogne on the English Channel, some 28 miles south-east of Folkestone. The history of the town dates back to Roman times when it first became a harbour, and it was to change hands many times through the ages, even becoming an English possession for six years after King Henry VIII took the town by siege in 1544. It was restored to France in 1550. Over the centuries Boulogne continued to develop and, by the beginning of the First World War, it was an established seaport and holiday resort.

In August 1914, the first units of Sir John French's army disembarked there and from this moment Boulogne became the main route for all troops entering France from England. As a result, the town became a major British base with much development centred on the old Camp de Boulogne, which had originally been built in 1801 as a base for Napoleon's army prior to the projected invasion of England. In 1804, the Colonne de la Grande Armée had been erected to commemorate the camp. The town was bombed in 1917 and 1918, although the nearest the German troops got to Boulogne was in 1914 when a few squadrons of cavalry came within 40 kilometres.

This area was to see bitter fighting in 1940. The 2. Panzer-Division advanced on Boulogne by way of Samer, which developed into an attack on 22nd May. Elements of the 20th Guards Brigade managed to beat off German assaults, and for the next three days a desperate resistance was put up, supported by the Royal Navy and French destroyers, until the ships were forced to withdraw. This left the French commander, General Pierre Lanquetot and a handful of men to fight on alone. The statue of Napoleon even being holed through the chest by the Royal Navy during the fighting! The town surrendered on the 25th. It was said by General Heinz Guderian that 'German tanks could not penetrate the old town walls but, by the use of a ladder from the kitchen of a nearby house and, with the help of an 8.8cm Flak gun, a breach was made in the wall of the cathedral.'

As a result of its close proximity to Britain, and its excellent harbour facilities, Boulogne was chosen to be one of the ports from which Operation 'Seelöwe', the German invasion of Britain, was to have been launched. It was at this point that many of the German defences were started both to protect and support these preparations. Very soon their construction included pens for a Schnellboot flotilla and the nearby siting of cross-Channel batteries. Over the next four years, under German occupation, the defences of the town continued to be enhanced. Some defences were built on the former French coastal positions, others were specially constructed by the Organisation Todt, occasionally installing weapons captured from the British during their evacuation. Throughout the next four years, Boulogne suffered a large number of air attacks from the Royal Air Force, and occasional bombardment from the British batteries in Kent.

Boulogne itself falls naturally into two parts: the business, commercial and residential area of the Basse-Ville surrounding the port, and the old town – the Haute-Ville – on a hill to the east containing the administrative centre, the cathedral and the walled 13th-century Citadel (sometimes referred to as the Château or Castle). This is the Rue de la Porte Neuve in May 1940, shortly before troops of the 2. Panzer-Division entered the city. In the background stands the cathedral which lies within the walls of the medieval fortifications. (ECPA)

THE DEFENDERS

While Canadian forces were fighting their way up the coast towards the Pas-de-Calais, the defences of Boulogne were further strengthened as a result of the Hitler Directive of 4th September stating that, like Le Havre, Boulogne, Dunkirk and the Calais area were to become 'Festungen' (Fortresses) and that they were to be defended to the last.

Colonel C. P. Stacey, the official Canadian historian, describes the defences and the battle which led to the capture of the town:

> *Boulogne was ringed on the landward side by a series of high hills which dominated all approaches. Mont Lambert on the east, in particular, rose 550 feet; and farther south the Herquelingue 'feature' was almost as high. These and other positions had been heavily fortified by a resourceful enemy, for Boulogne had been on Hitler's original list of 'fortresses'. The garrison was under an able and experienced senior officer, Generalleutnant Ferdinand Heim, who had served in Poland as Chief-of-Staff to General Guderian and had risen to command a corps in Russia. Its strength (estimated by Allied intelligence as between 5,500 and 7,000) was actually about 10,000. Its quality was not especially high, the 2,000 infantry consisting of a fortress machine gun battalion and two fortress infantry battalions, all made up of low-category men. A good part of the artillery and engineer personnel of the 64. Infanterie-Division were present. As at Le Havre, the Germans were strong in artillery, the guns including coast defence pieces up to 305mm (12-inch), of which, however, many could not fire landward, and at least 22 88mm guns, plus about nine 150mm howitzers belonging to the 64. Division. Apart from the dual-purpose 88s, there were few anti-tank guns.*

From the German point of view there was little cheer. The despair with which the garrison viewed the coming battle is reflected in the writings of one officer:

> 'September 7: Encircled in Boulogne. For days I knew that there was no getting out for us.
>
> September 9: Yesterday, late in the afternoon, enemy bombers attacked the forward positions. Sometimes one can despair of everything if one is at the mercy of the RAF without any protection.

September 11: All day long artillery fire in our outlying strong points and, in between, attacks by fighter-bombers. The morale of the troops is bad, and no wonder. They are mostly old married men and the situation is quite hopeless...

September 13: Alcohol is the only thing which can comfort anyone in our position ... This afternoon more heavy air attacks on the outer defences of Boulogne.

September 14: At the harbour command everyone is desperately gay and we try to drown all worries in alcohol.'

Boulogne had been given 'Fortress' status in Hitler's first list of 19th January, 1944, along with the other major ports of the Continental coast, including the U-Boat bases. Its commander was Generalleutnant Ferdinand Heim who had been appointed to the position on 5th August after spending several months on the retired list following his selection by Hitler as a scapegoat for the Soviet breakthrough on the Don River which led to the disastrous defeat at Stalingrad in February 1943. He arrived in 'Festung Boulogne' late in August to find that little had been done to prepare the fortress against a land attack. He had been instructed to build a defence zone some 15 kilometres thick, a task which would have taken several weeks and employed hundreds of troops. Heim had neither, so, as he later explained, 'I merely put a big red circle on the map to show that the work had been carried out.' (AP)

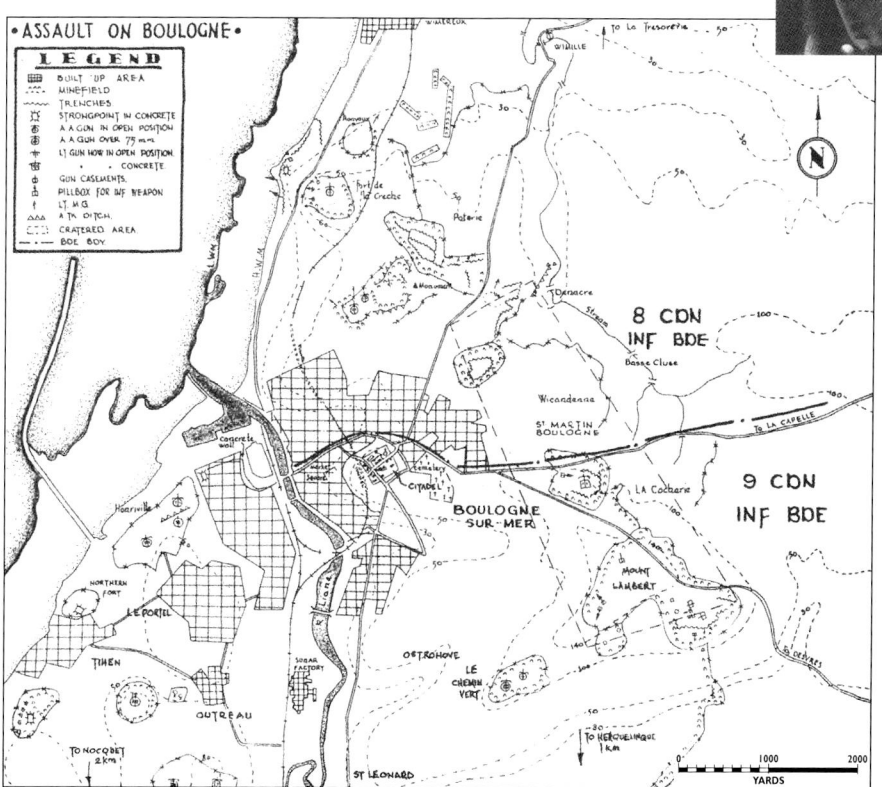

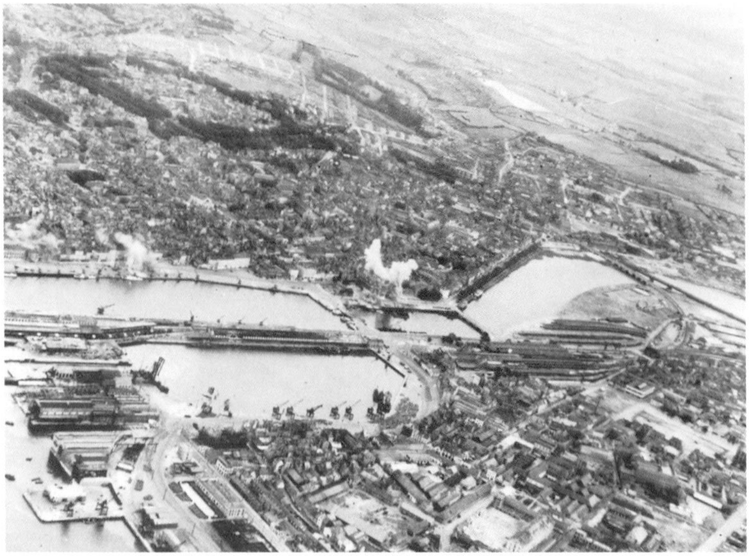

An air raid on the dock installations in 1942. Bombs can be seen exploding on the Quai Gambetta bordering the Port de Marée, and beside the Hôtel de la Poste just behind the Arrière Port. We are looking east with, in the left background, the tree-lined enclave marking the walls of the Citadel with the cathedral dome prominent at its northern end. (IWM)

One of the reasons for the regular attacks on Boulogne was the presence of what the Allies referred to as E-Boat pens ('E' ambiguously standing for Enemy) which had been built at the seaward end of the Appontement Nord. To confuse matters, the German classification for the same class of vessel was S-Boot, short for Schnellboot – 35-metre torpedo boats having a top speed of 42 knots, with a range of nearly 1,500 kilometres. These structures were concrete shelters for Schnellboote so should better be described as S-Boot pens. Their activities in 'Der Kanal' were controlled by Kapitän zur See Rudolf Petersen from his HQ at Wimereux just north of Boulogne. The S-Boote were a major threat to cross channel operations and had achieved one of their major victories in April 1944 when they sank two American tank landing ships off the Devon coast. This particular bombing raid took place the previous September, the same month when five B-17s of the Eighth Air Force joined 61 Wellingtons, 56 Stirlings and 10 Halifaxes of RAF Bomber Command in the first night raid of the war in which the Americans participated. The targets were two of the gun batteries at Boulogne but, in the event, the attack was a failure, both the target marking by *Oboe* and *Baillie Beam* Mosquitos and the bombing being inaccurate. (IWM)

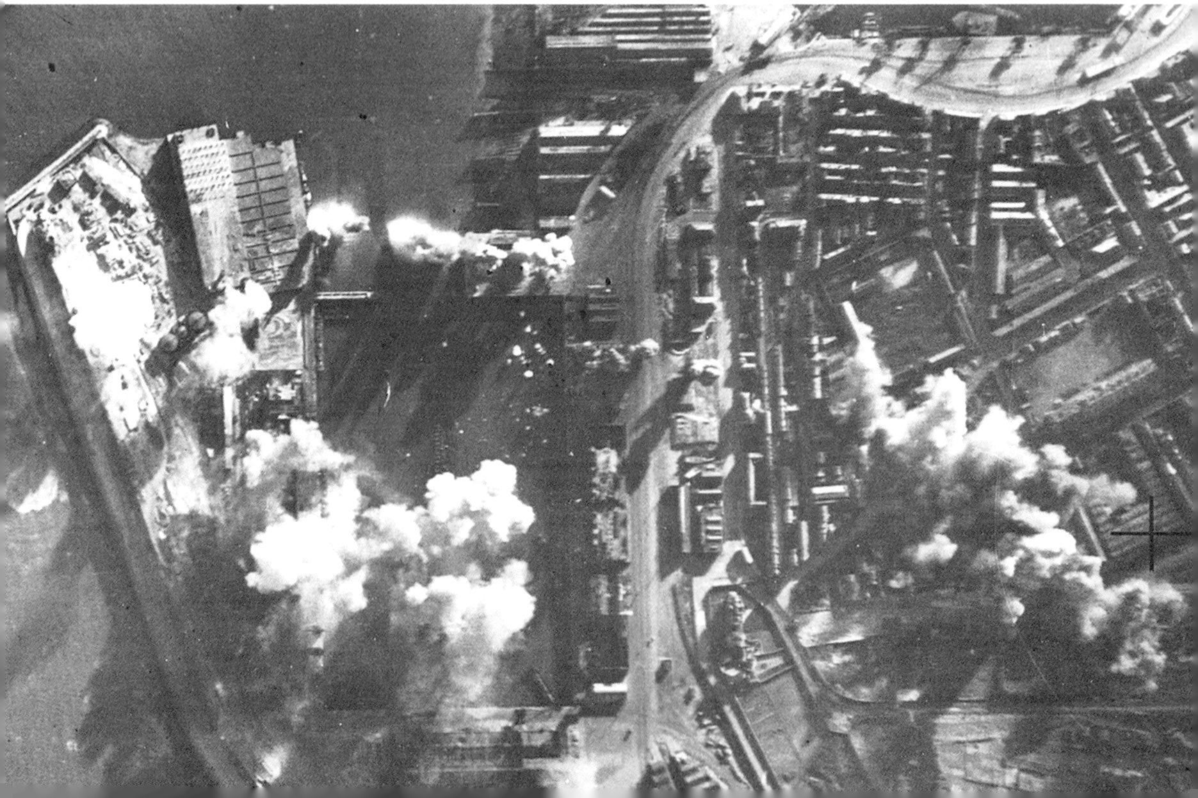

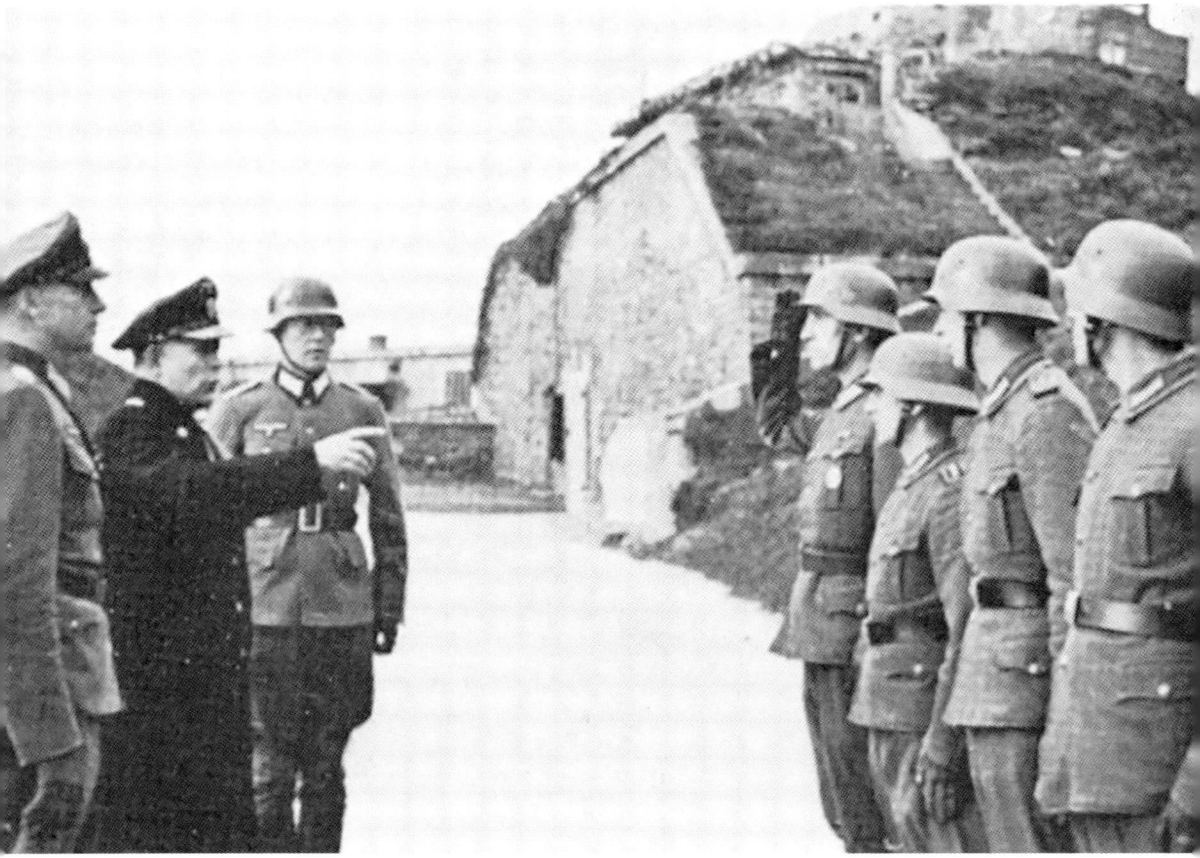

Ancient French fortifications found a new lease of life under their new owners. This is an inspection by Vize-Admiral Theodor Krancke, former captain of the 'pocket battleship' *Admiral Scheer*, later commander of Marine-Gruppenkommando West. At the fort on Mont de Coupes at Le Portel, the German Navy mounted three 13.8cm French guns.

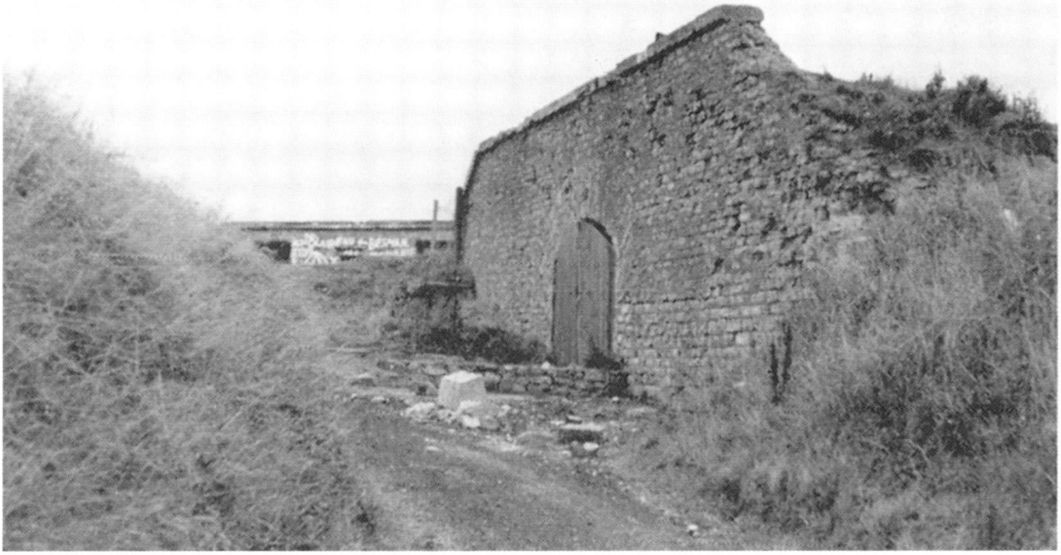

After General Crerar saw Montgomery on 9th September, he issued orders 'to proceed without delay to capture Boulogne, Dunkirk and Calais'. This was quite a tall order for an army which comprised two armoured and four infantry divisions, one of which could not be used for lack of transport, and which also had the task of driving German forces from the Scheldt and Walcheren. Montgomery then said that Dunkirk need not be captured, but instead 'masked' (contained by the 4th Special Service Brigade after its release from Le Havre). However, as it would be several days before artillery and AVRE assault vehicles from the British 79th Armoured Division could be brought up from Le Havre. It was the middle of the month before the attack on Boulogne could be mounted. These refugees were some of the 8,000 who left the city under German orders between 11th and 13th September. They were pictured by Canadian war photographer Donald Grant at La Capelle (on the N42 five kilometres east of the city), a spot which has hardly changed. (NAC)

THE ASSAULT FORCE

Advanced troops of Canadian II Corps had come up against the defences of Boulogne on 5th September. The town was far too strongly defended to be taken without a deliberate attack utilising heavy support and this meant delay. It is recorded that Lieutenant-General Guy Simonds, commanding II Corps, considered that it

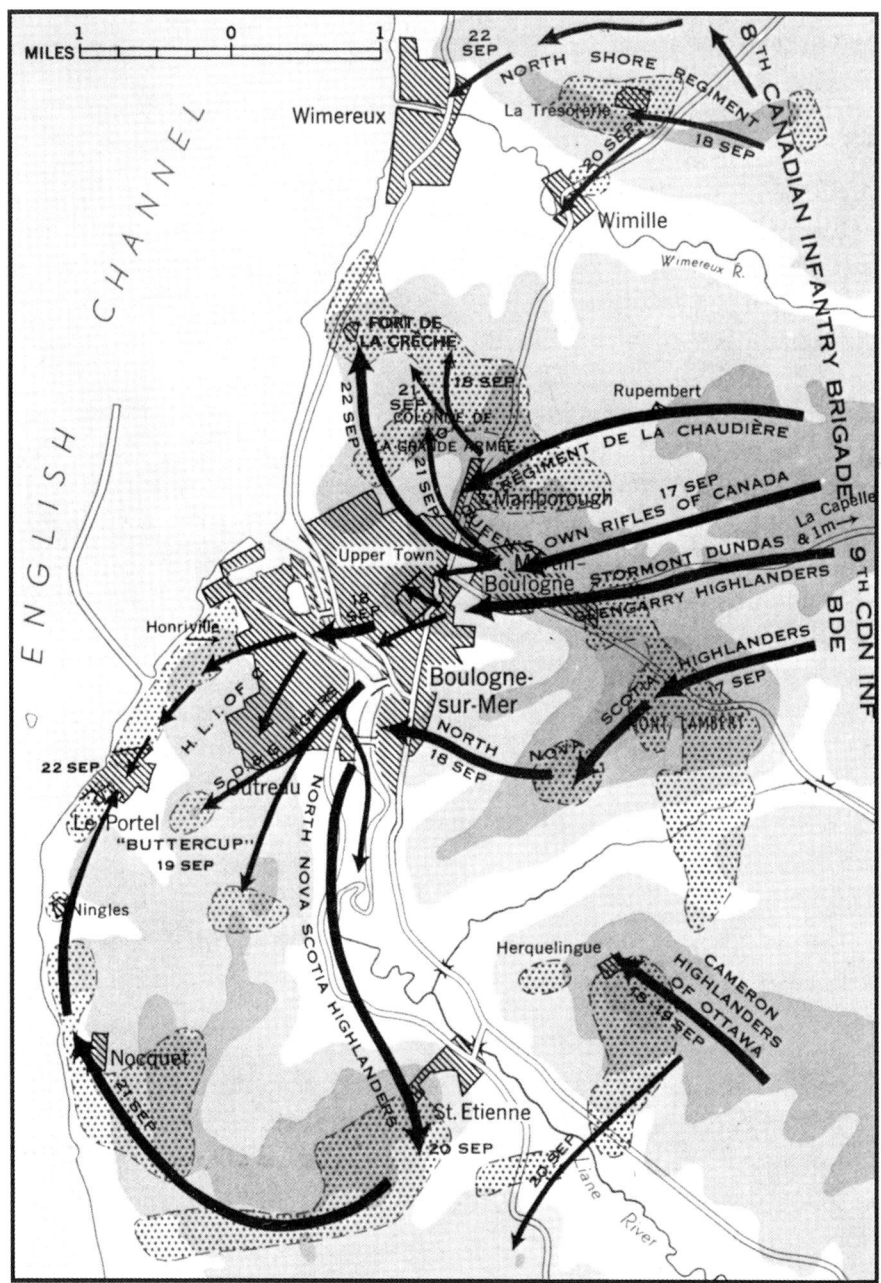

An overview of the battle plan from the official history shows how the main attack was to come in from the east, with the secondary attacks then occupying enemy positions one either flank.

Operation 'Wellhit' • 83

was vital to include 'bombers, Priests (armoured personnel carriers more commonly known as 'Kangaroos') and medium artillery' in the plan'. 'Other gadgets', by which he presumably meant the specialised armour of 79th Armoured Division, were desirable but not so much so as to necessitate postponing the attack to wait for them. However, RAF Bomber Command, the armoured carriers and a large proportion of the available artillery were all committed to the attack on Le Havre. Boulogne could not be attacked until Le Havre had fallen and these resources were freed. The distance between the two fortresses was roughly 135 miles by road.

The attack on Boulogne was allocated the codename Operation 'Wellhit'. The assault was to be executed by 3th Canadian Infantry Division in four phases. Major-General Daniel Spry, the division's GOC, intended to launch his main assault from the east against the general area of Mont Lambert, using the 8th and 9th Infantry Brigade Groups. They were to follow a heavy preliminary bombardment by aircraft and artillery. In the second phase, the two brigades would secure the centre of the built-up area and, it was hoped, seize a crossing over the Liane river before the bridges could be blown. The third phase would see the capture of outlying strong points at Fort de la Crèche, Outreau and Herquelingue, followed by the fourth phase: the capture of Nocquet on the coast and the heights of St Etienne.

Just in time to support the attack some elements of 79th Armoured Division had been able to be spared from the fighting at Le Havre. Two squadrons of the 1st Lothian and Border Yeomanry with mine-clearing Flail tanks had arrived, along with the 141st RAC (minus one squadron) equipped with flame-throwing Crocodile tanks. Two Royal Engineers assault squadrons with Churchill AVRE tanks were also brought up. The specialised armour was grouped under the command of 31st Tank Brigade commanded by Brigadier G. S. Knight.

The Army Commander, General Crerar, was clearly concerned that the capture of Boulogne should not go off half cocked. On 13th September he wrote to Field-Marshal Montgomery:

> 'While the rapid fall of Le Havre has favourable potential influences, it is most important that the effect so gained should not be more than lost by an unsuccessful attack on the next objective, Boulogne. I, therefore, want Simonds to button things up properly, taking a little more time, if necessary, in order to ensure a decisive assault.'

BOMBING SUPPORT

Key to Crerer's thinking was the bomber support and, in fact, this was the last part of the programme to be settled. A planned meeting with a representative of RAF Bomber Command did not materialise on 14th September, leading to a terse complaint emanating from HQ Canadian First Army, 'Whole affair now held up awaiting his arrival'. Exasperated by the lack of cooperation, General Simonds flew to Headquarters Allied Expeditionary Air Force at Versailles on the 15th. Accompanying him were his own Chief-of-Staff, Elliot Rodger and also that of Crerar, Clarence Mann. They took with them the Senior Air Staff Officer of No. 84 Group, Air Vice Marshal Leslie Brown. In what must have been a lively exchange the question of air support at both Boulogne and Calais was addressed. Initial discussions were not particularly satisfactory. Two air vice-marshals, one of whom was from Bomber Command, were reluctant 'to use more than 300-400 RAF [heavy] bombers for each port', arguing that such an attack could be better achieved by medium bombers. It is clear that Crerer was unsatisfied with the response and the discussion rapidly escalated. Air Chief Marshals Tedder, Harris and Leigh-Mallory, respectively Deputy Supreme Commander, AOC-in-C Bomber Command, and the AOC Allied Expeditionary Force were called in to resolve the matter. The Corps Commander seized the opportunity and put his case to them. All three 'agreed with little hesitation that if Boulogne and Calais were to be captured forthwith and air support was necessary, then it should be given in full measure'. The details were worked out at once and the plan 'buttoned up'. Next day, General Spry announced that the 'Wellhit' D-Day would be 17th September. Thus the assault on Boulogne was to be staged on the same day as Operation Market Garden, the much more grandiose airborne operation aimed at capturing Eindhoven, Nijmegen and Arnhem in Holland.

SOFTENING-UP

During the final stage of preparation, particularly after the fall of Le Havre, the tactical air forces were directed against Boulogne. All told, there were 49 attacks, before the assault, by mediums, fighter-bombers and rocket-firing Typhoons. Their main targets were battery positions; these were also engaged by the gradually growing force of artillery deployed around Boulogne. However, ammunition shortages prevented heavy counter-battery fire before the actual day of the assault. Ultimately, 328 guns were used against the fortress: those of five field, seven medium, three heavy artillery regiments, along with two regiments of heavy anti-aircraft artillery. The British 9th Army Group Royal Artillery and the divisional artillery of the 51st (Highland) Division, both of which had hurried up from Le Havre, joined with the Canadian gunners in this operation. Since this great force of artillery was supporting the Canadian 3rd Division, the responsibility for co-ordinating and directing the effort rested mainly upon the 3rd Division's artillery commander, Brigadier Stanley Todd.

There was potent artillery help also from across the Channel. The Brigadier Royal Artillery, Canadian First Army (Brigadier H. O. N. Brownfield) flew to England and arranged for the mammoth guns on the South Foreland, east of Dover, to fire on the German cross-Channel batteries in the Calais–Cap Gris-Nez area, to prevent them from interfering with the attack on Boulogne. Two 14-inch guns (nicknamed 'Winnie' and 'Pooh') manned by the Royal Marine Siege Regiment, and two 15-inch manned by the 540th Coast Regiment, RA, came into action, firing with air observation. After some preliminary shooting on the 16th, their fire continued actively and accurately into the 17th. The German battery positions were hit repeatedly and one of the 15-inch guns scored a direct hit on one of the casemates at the Noires Mottes battery near Sangatte. The Germans referred to this position as Batterie Lindemann, which housed three 406mm guns), the range being about 42,000 yards, or over 23 miles. The 15-inch guns fired all day until their old barrels were so worn that they could no longer reach the French coast. The 14-inch were in action again on 19th and 20th September.

D-DAY

At 0825-hrs on 17th September, the first aircraft from Bomber Command appeared over Boulogne. An officer who was watching from high ground south of the city described the scene: 'The bombers approached us head on; suddenly, huge bursts of dust and smoke plumed out on the slopes of Mount Lambert . . . Over the peak of Mount Lambert appeared a tight concentration of low (artillery) air bursts, designed to keep the flak crews there below ground . . . A later wave of bombers, directed on the peak of the mount was preceded by a Pathfinder which dropped a white smoke marker. The artillery seemed also to lay smoke here. A swarm of planes then materialised out of the sky as before, and once again huge clouds of smoke blotted out the shape of the hill-top.'

Mont Lambert dominated the high ground to the east of the city. Subjected to a heavy bombardment from both bomb and shell, while the lighter constructions were destroyed, the reinforced concrete bunkers and blockhouses survived relatively intact. (IWM)

The hill is now dominated by a massive broadcasting aerial though a nest of bunkers still occupy the summit.

In this single attack, Bomber Command dropped 3,232 tons of bombs on Boulogne. A total of 540 Lancasters, 212 Halifaxes and 40 Mosquitoes took part. In spite of the artillery fire directed on the flak positions, two aircraft were lost. An RAF group captain was with Brigadier John Rockingham (CO of the 9th Infantry Brigade) in his tactical headquarters dug in on his brigade's start-line.

Operation 'Wellhit' • 87

The 9th Brigade advanced to La Cocherie supported by two AVREs, while another troop from the 87th Assault Squadron attacked Mont Lambert. It proved a very difficult nut to crack as Generalleutnant Heim realised that if the dominant feature was captured by the Canadians, it would effectively remove his ability to defend the port. Although the blockhouses had been battered, they are still basically intact.

This bunker on the south-east side of the hill covered the road from Baincthun. In this case, the frontal damage to the aperture could well have been caused by one of the petard-armed AVREs. (IWM)

Post-war demolition has further removed part of the canopy and the steel shield.

He was in radio communication with the master bomber overhead and was able to pass to him the brigadier's confirmation that the markers put down by the pathfinder aircraft were on precisely the right points. This was 'close co-operation' at its best.

As at Le Havre, the precise results of this bombardment are a matter of discussion. Generalleutnant Heim claimed that 'amongst personnel, casualties were almost negligible' and that there was little effect on permanent installations. After the battle, British operational researchers found that only a relatively small proportion of the enemy's guns had actually been destroyed or damaged. The extensive cratering also impeded armoured vehicles supporting the ground attack. However, like in Le Havre, ample evidence suggested that the bombing seriously disrupted the defenders' communications and shook their morale. A German who had been in an underground bunker during the attacks remarked that it was 'like being in the bottom of a cocktail-shaker.' The investigators noted that positions within the limits of the heavy bomber targets were captured much more rapidly than those outside. Moreover, the bombing certainly gave, as always, a fillip to the spirits of our own infantry which was no small factor in their success. Headquarters First Army, commenting on the researchers' report some months later, remarked: 'Despite the proved lack of material effect of ground or air bombardment on the defences, it is considered that both the RAF and the artillery bombardment were extremely effective in neutralising the enemy defences.'

THE ASSAULT

The 8th Infantry Brigade (Brigadier K. G. Blackader) began their assault on the on the right flank, the 9th (Brigadier J. M. Rockingham) on the left. H-Hour was 0955-hrs – the moment when the last bomb fell on Target 1. It was considered important, if at all possible, to capture the extreme northern end of the German defended area before the main attack went in. The strong points about La Trèsorerie and Wimille appeared to present an excessive danger to the attacking force. A coastal battery on the hill at La Trèsorerie [Batterie Friedrich-August] mounted three 305mm (12-inch) guns and, though these could not fire landward, the extensive strongpoint around them boasted a commanding position. Accordingly, the North Shore (New Brunswick) Regiment was to attack it at 0925-hrs after half an hour's artillery preparation. The evident assumption that 30 minutes would suffice to clear the area turned out to be somewhat optimistic.

After making slight progress, the attack was checked in minefields covered by airburst fire from light artillery. The North Shore in fact did not clear all its objectives until 19th September. Nevertheless, the goal was partially achieved in that it seems to have kept the Germans on the position occupied enough to prevent them from interfering with the main attack.

The task of the 8th Brigade's main body was to deal with the enemy's defences between Mont Lambert and La Trèsorerie, in the vicinity of Marlborough and St Martin–Boulogne. Immediately after the bombing, Le Règiment de la Chaudière advanced against Marlborough. En route they occupied an intact radar station in the hamlet of Rupembert; and by nightfall they were consolidating in Marlborough itself. On the brigade's left flank, to the south, The Queen's Own Rifles of Canada were directed against St Martin–Boulogne. By 1100-hrs they had captured the railway station there and by evening they were close to the 'citadel' of Boulogne. Throughout the brigade area, shell-fire and minefields were the main hindrances to advance.

While these operations were proceeding on the northern flank, the 9th Brigade assaulted the Mont Lambert feature, moving forward the moment the Bomber Command attack had ceased. Tanks of the 10th Armoured Regiment (the Fort Garry Horse) led the way, the infantry riding into battle in Kangaroos and half-tracks which were followed by AVREs of the 87th Assault Squadron, RE. Flails had also been provided to clear paths through the minefields but when the attack went in, the enemy's artillery prevented this relatively vulnerable equipment from coming into action.

On the right, along the main road from La Capelle, the Stormont, Dundas and Glengarry Highlanders led the assault in 'galloping Kangaroos under a tremendous barrage of artillery'. The artillery actually fired timed programmes, prolonging the neutralising effect of the bombing and enabling the infantry to reach their first objectives with diminished opposition. When minefields stopped the Kangaroos, the Glengarrians continued on foot. They took only 45 minutes to capture their first objectives. By this time, however, the German batteries had recovered sufficiently to bring down accurate fire from their commanding positions on the slopes of Mont Lambert and nearby hills. Although the shelling made movement almost impossible, men of the 18th Field Company, RCE, performed an outstanding feat by clearing a vital route through the mines by hand.

Meanwhile, the North Nova Scotia Highlanders ran into heavy opposition when they attacked the main fortifications of the

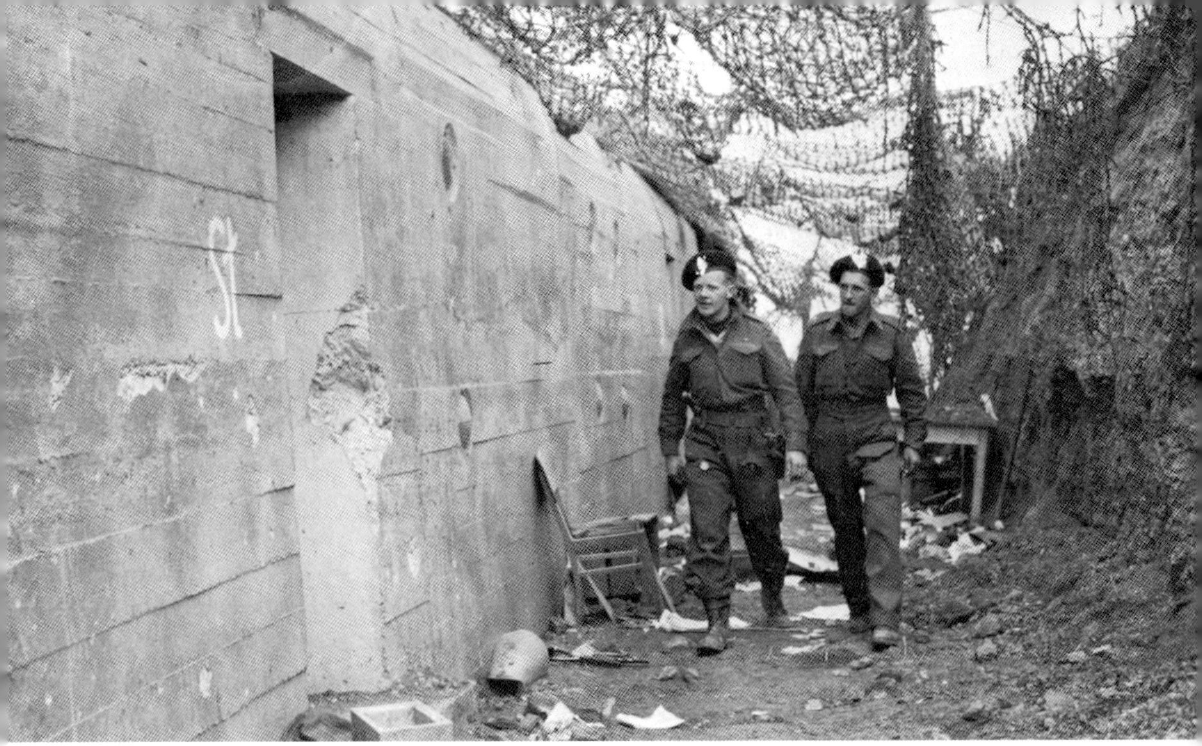

Eddie Worth, wartime photographer with Associated Press, visited Mont Lambert on 22nd September when he pictured Private R. Hallahan of Montreal with Corporal T. E. Warren of Winnipeg outside a troop shelter.

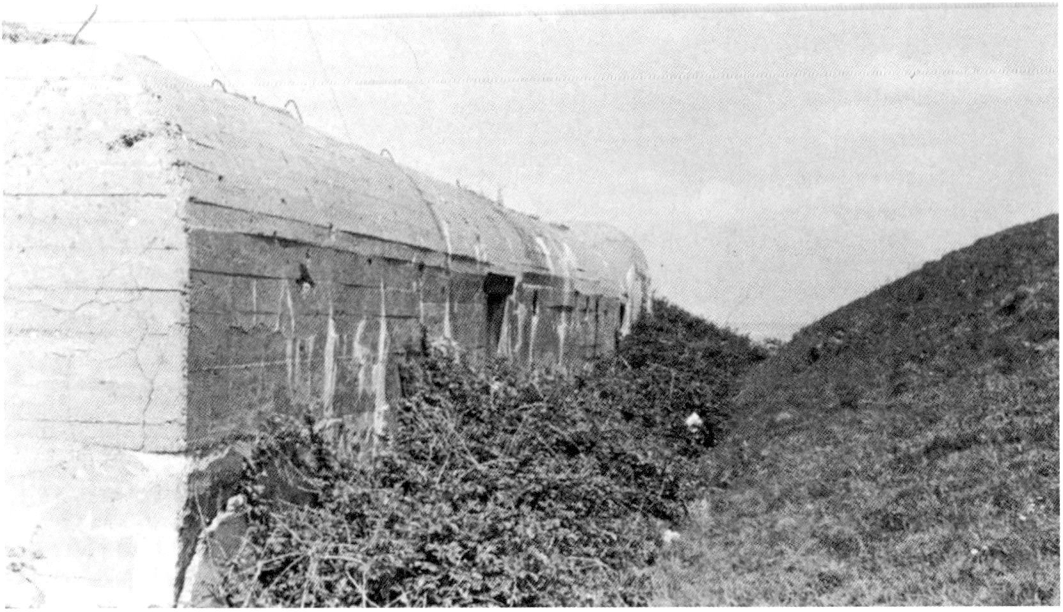

Ian Galbraith found the same bunker, its entrance choked with foliage.

Mont Lambert feature. Both sides had appreciated the importance of this dominating ground; Generalleutnant Heim believed that penetration in that sector 'would make defence of the port impossible'. He claimed, however, that his defensive preparations here had not been completed when 'Wellhit' began. The North Nova Scotias were transported in Kangaroos as far as the minefields. Thereafter, their

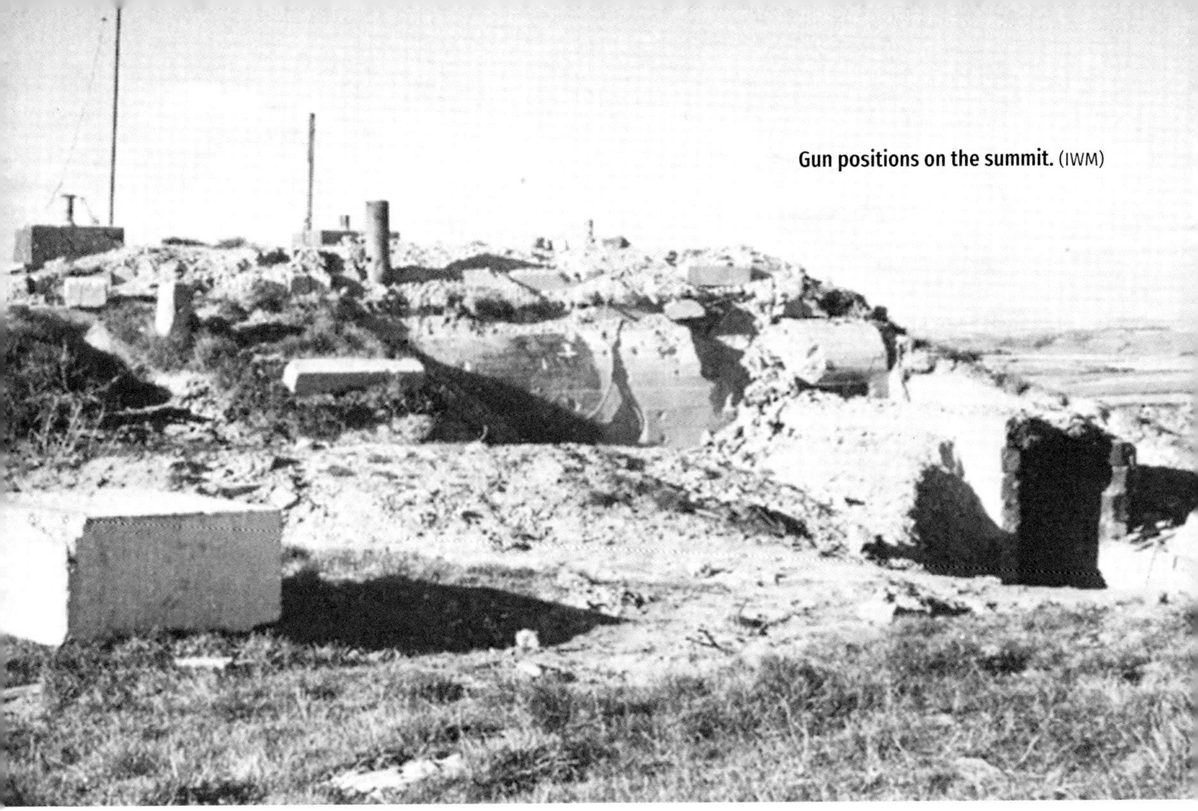

Gun positions on the summit. (IWM)

The security fence surrounding the broadcasting station can be seen on the left.

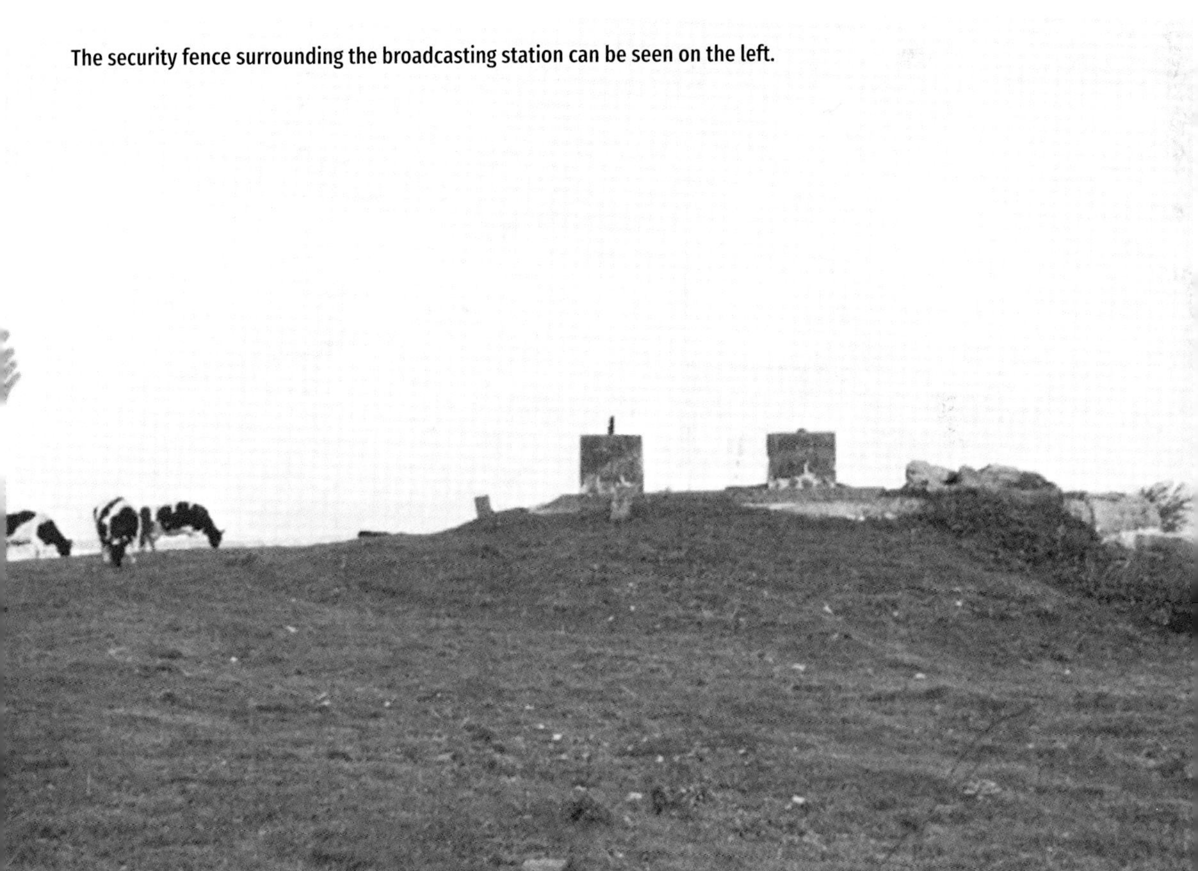

The N42 – the main axis route from the east which formed the boundary between the 8th and 9th Brigades – on 16th September. Here, Donald Grant pictured two aspects of the operations being conducted at that time. A Churchill SBG bridge-layer of number 3 Troop, 81st Assault Squadron, RE, which appears to be named 'Flint II', and prisoners being brought in from Mont Lambert. (NAC). Three armoured assault columns, under the 9th Brigade, but comprising mainly 79th Armoured Division components, were to press forward into the city to seize bridges over the River Liane, and they set off in the late afternoon of the 17th.

Although the road has been widened at this point, the château remains almost unchanged. From here, Boulogne 'Centre Ville' is six kilometres down the road.

forward progress up the hill was delayed by machine gun fire from pillboxes which had survived the bombing. These were overcome with the help of AVREs and the hard ascent continued. 'Towards night, Crocodiles and Flails were able to come up and the area was steadily cleared.' By the day's end, a great part of Mont Lambert was in Canadian hands.

From the German standpoint, this diary entry by the anonymous officer previously quoted recorded:

> 'September 17: It is nine months today since I last went on leave. What a good time I had. And today what a contrast. I was just ready to go to breakfast when we had to run for shelter and we have been there ever since. The bombardment by bombers and artillery was terrific. It is four o'clock in the afternoon now. I am looking at your pictures, my loved ones. I am quiet now and resigned to my fate whatever it may be. Farewell, my dear ones, I pray to God that He may protect and guide you . . . All afternoon a heavy artillery barrage fell on our positions. We could not move. Then we heard tanks approaching and had to surrender. It is a wonder that we are still alive . . .'

Arrangements had been made for three armoured assault teams of the British 31st Tank Brigade to drive into Boulogne. Each team was composed of one troop of Flails, two troops of Crocodiles and one half troop of AVREs, together with one platoon of Canadian infantry. This marked the end of the first phase, which was

Operation 'Wellhit' • 95

intended to be completed by the seizure of the important bridges over the Liane river in the heart of the city. The Glengarrians provided the infantry component for two of the assault teams and these reached the Liane early on the 18th only to find the bridges blown. The third team, operating with the North Nova Scotias, was similarly frustrated.

Thus, at the end of the first day, a considerable wedge had been driven into the enemy's fortifications in the Highland Brigade's sector, while in the 8th's good progress had been made. At the extreme north of the position, the North Shore Regiment had a foothold in the La Trèsorerie strong point. All along the line, however, the operation had gone more slowly than forecast. A paper produced at the HQ of First Army on 15th September highlights that they had assumed that Boulogne would fall in one day and that Calais could be attacked on the 19th.

The 18th, however, saw further solid progress. In the 8th Brigade sector, the North Shore completed the capture of the gun positions at La Trèsorerie; the Chaudière pushed on to the vicinity of the Colonne de la Grande Armèe where there was hard fighting. The Queen's Own advanced through the northern outskirts of the city. In the 9th Brigade area, the North Nova Scotias completed the capture of Mont Lambert. The Glengarrians, accompanied by AVREs, reached the so-called citadel in the centre of Boulogne. This was actually the 'upper town', perched on a limestone hill overlooking the port and surrounded by high walls. It soon succumbed to a combination of modern methods of assault and a stroke of luck that could have come out of a story book. One of the Glengarrians company commanders, Major J. G. Stothart, came across a French civilian who showed him a 'secret tunnel' leading to the interior. Stothart took a platoon into the passage. The regimental history records, 'At the same time, the Churchills wheeled up, raking the ramparts with Besa [machine gun] fire, and prepared to place petards against the portcullis. The gate was effectively blown in. At once, a host of white flags waved from the walls. To add to the confusion, Major Stothart had by now appeared in the midst of the besieged fort, utterly astonishing its "defenders".'

About 200 prisoners were taken, including sixteen officers. The Highland Light Infantry of Canada, coming up from reserve, scrambled across the Liane in the evening by using the remains of a half-demolished bridge in the middle of the city. The 18th Field Company then set to work to improvise repairs to the bridge with timber, and had it open for light vehicles by 0430-hrs on the 19th.

Bomb craters and rubble hindered the advance but, by nightfall, eight tanks from Column 'A' had succeeded in reaching the Citadel. At 0630-hrs the next morning (18th), the attack began, one Sherman destroying machine gun positions on the walls. With a bullet hole in his windscreen, Donald Grant follows the route through the eastern outskirts towards the Citadel the following day. (NAC)

This is still the N42 although at this point it is called the Rue de St Omer.

Operation 'Wellhit' • 97

Reaching the Rue de la Porte Neuve (see page 77), Don Grant is just in time to picture captured troops being marched away to the east. Over 200 prisoners had been taken in the Citadel which fell after two AVREs fired petard charges at the main gate to demolish the barricade protecting it. At the same time, Canadian infantry appeared within the walls, having been shown a secret entrance by a Frenchman. (NAC)

Rue de la Porte Neuve at the junction with Rue de St Omer and Rue de Calais, which has now been re-named Avenue de Général de Gaulle.

The capture of the upper town and the crossing of the Liane marked the end of the second phase. While the 8th Brigade continued its operations to subdue the German defences north of the port, the 9th turned south to deal with equally stubborn strong points in the Outreau peninsula. On 19th September, the HLI pressed forward here from its Liane bridgehead. The opposition was very heavy: 'Murderous fire came from all directions which was heavier than the battalion has yet experienced'. It had 64 casualties and four supporting Flails were knocked out. The Glengarrians took up the struggle in the afternoon with the help of tanks, AVREs and Wasps (flame-throwing carriers). They seized the village of Outreau, after extricating themselves from a minefield, and captured many prisoners, 'including perhaps 30 black Senegalese complete with fez'.

Between Outreau and the open Channel was a hill, about 250 feet high, capped with a German battery of six 8.8cm and four 2cm guns. The Glengarrians assaulted this formidable position, known in the plan as 'Buttercup' aided by heavy artillery concentrations. 'The infantry, following the fire closely, swarmed over the hill with bayonets and grenades before the last rounds had fallen.' 'Buttercup' contributed another 185 prisoners to the already bulging cages in the rear areas.

The North Nova Scotia Highlanders completed the next phase in the Outreau peninsula with the assistance of the divisional machine gun battalion, the Cameron Highlanders of Ottawa. After containing the enemy on the southern flank during the initial operations, the Camerons had successfully assaulted the German position on top of the very high hill at Herquèlingue on the night of 18th/19th September. However, when the North Nova Scotias advanced on the 20th, they came under fire from the lower slopes of the feature. About 400 German soldiers had remained hidden in the underground passages of Herquèlingue while the Camerons occupied the casemates on the summit. Some tank fire from the Fort Garry Horse quelled the opposition and, next day, this large force came marching out to surrender (General Spry christened this 'the bargain basement incident'). The North Nova Scotias had continued their advance to capture the village of St Etienne and subsequently turned north along the coast to deal with the remaining defences at Nocquet, Ningles and Le Portel.

While the 9th Brigade was completing its tasks in the Outreau peninsula the 8th was reducing the last German defences on the northern outskirts of Boulogne. In this area, the focal points of resistance were Wimille, Fort de la Crèche and Wimereux.

The 9th Brigade soon established its headquarters in the old Citadel – a building which had seen more than its fair share of history. Dating from the 13th century, it had been here after the First World War that the coffin bearing the remains of Britain's Unknown Warrior transited on his way to London. Brigadier-General L. J. Wyatt, GOC British troops in France and Flanders, had been tasked with selecting the Warrior from four exhumed bodies, each from unmarked graves of soldiers who died early in the war. This was decided so that decomposition would mean the bodies were completely unrecognisable. They were examined for any identifying marks, then each one was covered in a union flag. After the stroke of midnight on 7th December, 1920, Wyatt made his selection and the following day the chosen body was moved from St Pol the 60-odd kilometres to Boulogne. There it rested overnight in the Chapelle Ardente in the Citadel until the morning of 10th November when it was carried from the chapel for the next stage in his journey to Whitehall.

Signalman F. R. J. Savage of the 9th Brigade, Royal Canadian Corps of Signals, looks at the damaged plaque which recorded the event. (NAC)

Ian Galbraith, examines the new tablet which now replaces the old.

On the 20th, Eddie Worth pictured scenes inside the city as Canadian forces pressed on towards the port area. 'The Battle of Boulogne has entered the final phase', ran the 1944 caption. 'Canadians, creeping from doorway to doorway, are slowly but surely edging towards the remnants of the German garrison making their last stand. The town has taken terrific punishment from air and artillery. Machine-gunning and shelling continue to be fierce.'

This is the Grand Rue which leads from the Citadel to the port, although it is now one-way, heading up the hill.

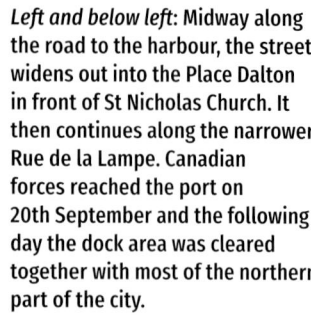

Left and below left: Midway along the road to the harbour, the street widens out into the Place Dalton in front of St Nicholas Church. It then continues along the narrower Rue de la Lampe. Canadian forces reached the port on 20th September and the following day the dock area was cleared together with most of the northern part of the city.

Above right and below right: Ian was fortunate in being able to gain vantage points virtually the same as those used by Eddie Worth in 1944.

On 19th September, the North Shore moved against Wimille; they met stubborn resistance but captured the village, together with many prisoners, the following morning. From this time, the momentum of the attack slowed as some of Generalleutnant Heim's best troops fought tenaciously for their last strong points.

Since Fort de la Crèche was strongly held, the 8th Brigade screened it with smoke and attacked the town of Wimereux on the 21st.

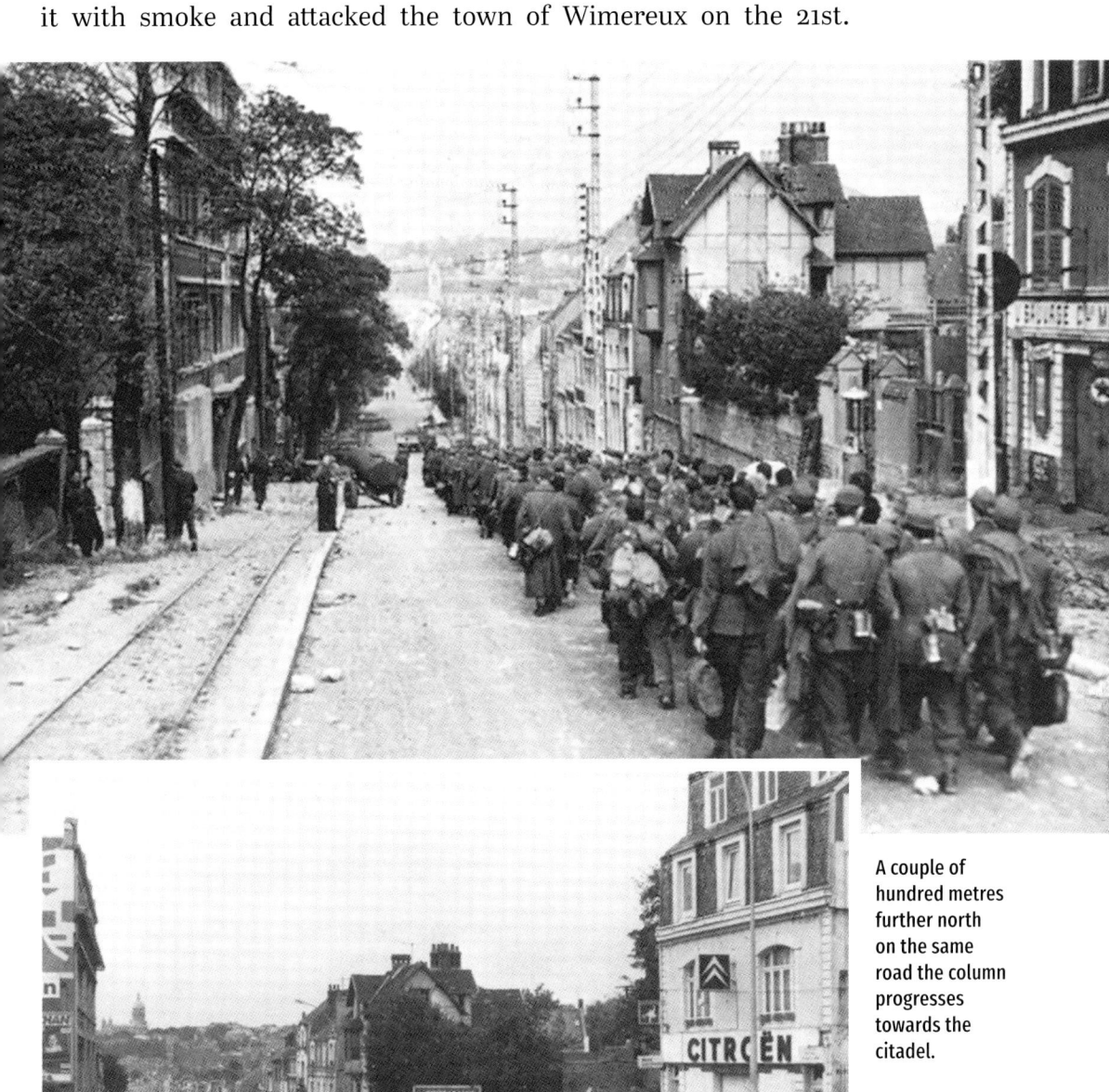

A couple of hundred metres further north on the same road the column progresses towards the citadel.

Operation 'Wellhit' • 103

Fort de la Crèche was captured early on 22nd September after a massive artillery and air bombardment had failed to dislodge the garrison. It was a formidable position with both large calibre naval guns and close-support weapons. (IWM)

Lieutenant-Colonel J. E. Anderson of the North Shore was reluctant to employ heavy bombardment against a target which he knew contained many civilians. Accordingly, only one field regiment and some captured light German guns engaged the defences while the infantry gradually penetrated the eastern portion of the town. Effective close support was given by a battery of the 3rd Anti-Tank Regiment, RCA, which silenced machine guns in the railway station. Fortunately, the town's main defences faced seawards and the North Shore were able to complete the capture of Wimereux on the 22nd, receiving a warm welcome from the population.

By this time the formidable Fort de la Crèche had also fallen. This 'northern anchor of the main fortifications' was an old French work which the Germans had modernised and greatly strengthened. When 'Wellhit' began, its armament included six naval guns (two 210mm and four 105mm) as well as lighter field and Flak pieces. The defenders' morale was noticeably higher than had been that of the remainder of the garrison. On 21st September, patrols of the Queen's Own Rifles and the Chaudière probed the outer works and obtained valuable information in spite of a strong reaction from the defenders. During the afternoon of the same day, some 78 medium bombers of No. 2 Group, RAF, attacked the fort. These preliminaries proved their worth when the Queen's Own advanced the following morning. With the assistance of a captured German artillery piece, they quickly subdued the now disheartened garrison; Fort de la Crèche surrendered at 0750-hrs It was reported that some 500 prisoners were taken in this stronghold.

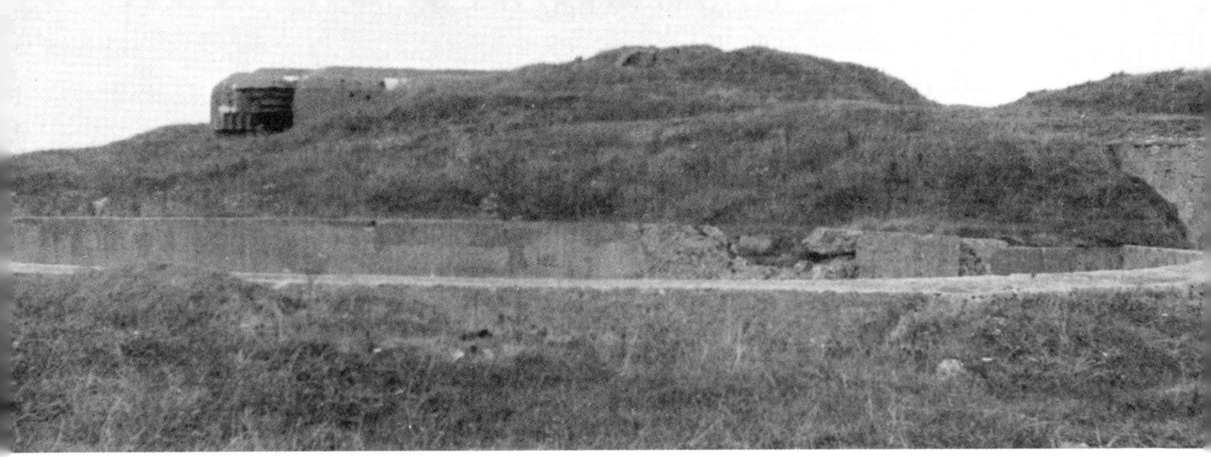

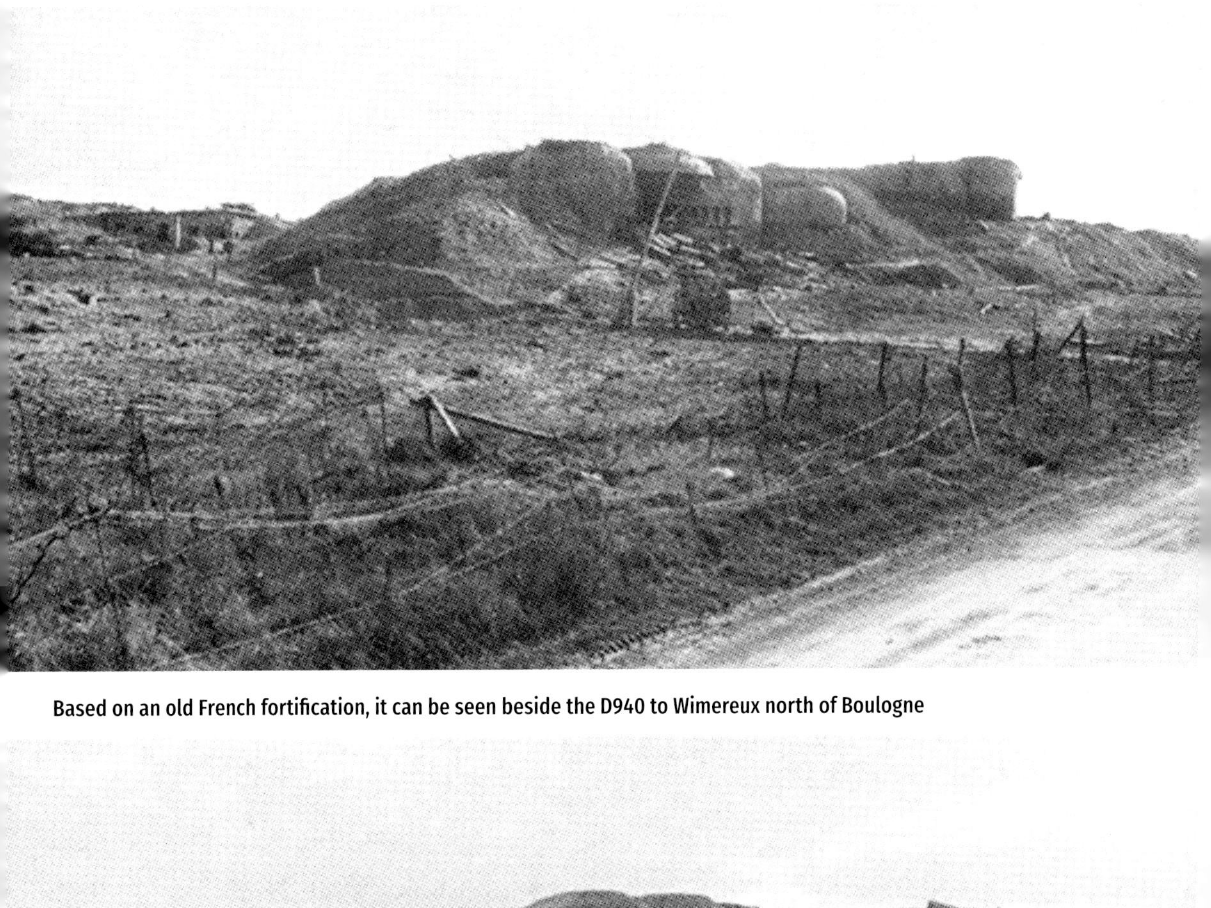

Based on an old French fortification, it can be seen beside the D940 to Wimereux north of Boulogne

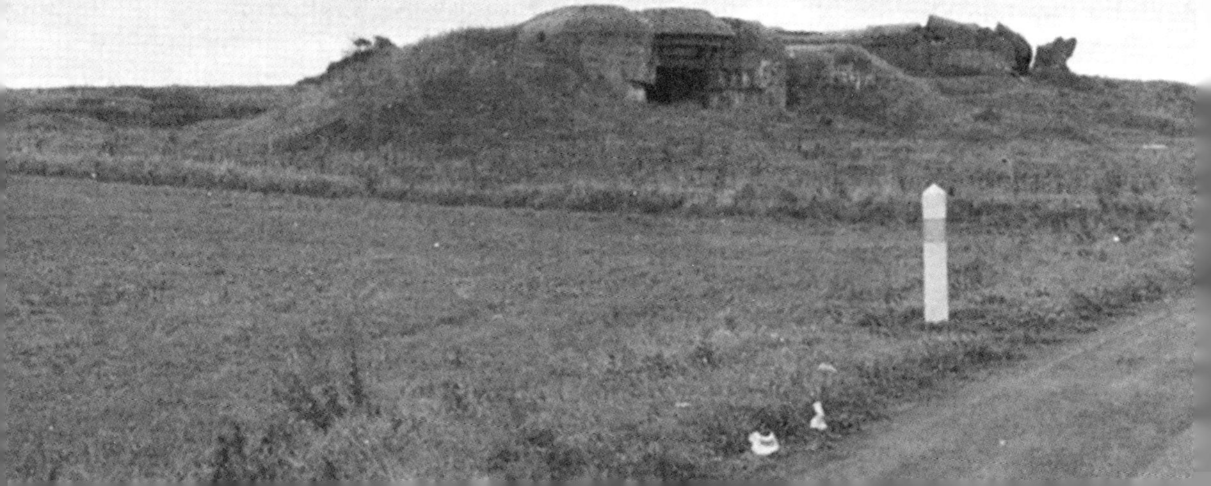

THE END

Operation 'Wellhit' ended on the afternoon of 22nd September in the Outreau peninsula. Scout cars with loudspeakers impressed the futility of further resistance on the garrison at Le Portel. There were two strong points here. The northern one fell first; then, just as the 9th Brigade and a squadron of the 10th Armoured Regiment were about to assault the southerly position, the enemy hoisted the white flag. Generalleutnant Heim surrendered to Brigadier Rockingham at 1630-hrs and the last fighting ceased after the German commander sent a cease-fire order to a detachment isolated on the harbour mole, which had fought a single 8.8cm gun to the bitter end.

Six days had been consumed in the operations against Boulogne at a juncture when time was of utmost importance. The delay aside, the results were gratifying. The Canadians took 9,517 prisoners, including 250 wounded, whilst their own losses were calculated as 634 killed, wounded and missing. Those of the six infantry battalions that bore the brunt amounted to 462, the 9th Brigade's (247) being very slightly higher than the 8th's (215). The heaviest loss fell upon the Highland Light Infantry of Canada (97 casualties, 18 of them fatal) and the North Nova Scotia Highlanders (96 casualties, 27 fatal).

Left and opposite above: Brigadier John Rockingham is pictured accepting the surrender of Generalleutnant Heim at the more southerly of the two forts – Le Portel – where the German garrison commander had moved his command post after the position at Mont Lambert had fallen. The number of Germans killed during the defence of Boulogne is not known, but Generalleutnant Heim said casualties were astonishingly light. Although the garrison troops had given an oath to defend the fortress 'to the end of my life and that of the last man under me', after the war Heim said that 'I felt I could lay down my charge with a clear conscience when I decided the situation was hopeless from a military standpoint. It is difficult for us Western people to sacrifice our lives when the situation is hopeless', he explained, 'and that is the main reason for my troops surrendering rather than dying in their bunkers. The further east you go the less important death becomes. The Japanese have no fear of death at all, and the Russians have almost none. In England and America life is very precious, and everything is done in wartime to preserve it and prevent its needless waste. We Germans stand in the middle.' (AP & IWM)

The front of the fort at Le Portel still shows signs of the heavy bombardment. In the far distance lies Cap Griz-Nez, the next objective in the Canadian drive up the coast.

'The bargain basement.' On the morning of 21st September the German officer commanding the garrison at Herquélingue (south-east of the city) surrendered, bringing with him about 500 men in all. They were to come out over a set route between midday and 1300 hrs along the N1 – the Route de Paris. Don Grant pictured the column as it negotiated rubble from a bridge which, the caption says, was blown to obstruct Allied vehicles. (NAC)

The Roule de Paris in 1997. At this time one of the bridges piers was still in place, though today they have been subsumed by modernisation..

The Jardin des Tintelleries became a temporary holding area for many of the 9,500-odd prisoners who had surrendered.

Located just north-west of the Citadel, off the Rue Dutertre, the garden has now adopted an air of utilitarianism following the loss of the ornamental bandstands. (IWM)

Operation 'Wellhit' • 109

On 14th October the victory was celebrated in what is now the Place de la Resistance – a square little changed in the intervening 50 years. (IWM)

Next came the job of clearing up the destruction from the thousands of tons of bombs dropped in and around the city. Air Marshal Sir Arthur Coningham, AOC of the RAF's Second Tactical Air Force, was sceptical of the 'wasteful destruction of habitations and the unavoidable heavy loss of life of friendly nationals in the occupied areas'. Experience of heavy bombing in Sicily, at Cassino, and, more recently, at Caen, St Lô and Villers-Bocage, led to, as he phrased it, 'the damaged areas [being] actually improved as centres of defence by snipers and special detachments of the enemy.' And, as occurred at Boulogne, the ground over which the troops had to cross was so choked with rubble and craters that it impeded and even halted the advance of the armoured columns. (IWM)

This is the Quai Gambetta where, in spite of the devastation, the bunkers were still intact. A Canadian soldier still appears wary of hidden snipers two days after the surrender. (IWM)

Due to the total devastation, the whole of this quay was rebuilt after the war. Air Marshal Coningham wrote in his official post-war despatch that 'the bombing of friendly towns during the campaign, and the insistence by the Army Commanders that it was a military necessity, caused me more personal worry and sorrow than I can say. My resistance, apart from humanitarian grounds, was due to a conviction, since confirmed, that in most cases we were harming Allies and ourselves eventually more than the enemy. I thought, also, of the good name of our forces, and particularly of the Air Force. It is a sad fact that the Air Forces will get practically all blame for destruction which, in almost every case, was due to Army demands. On many occasions, owing to the organisation of command, I was over-ruled and then came the "blotting" by strategic bombers who, on their experience with German targets, tended to over-hit. Ample factual evidence will now be forthcoming, and I hope that, in future, it will not be thought that the sight and sound of bombers, and their uplift effect on morale, is proportional to the damage they do to the enemy.' (IWM)

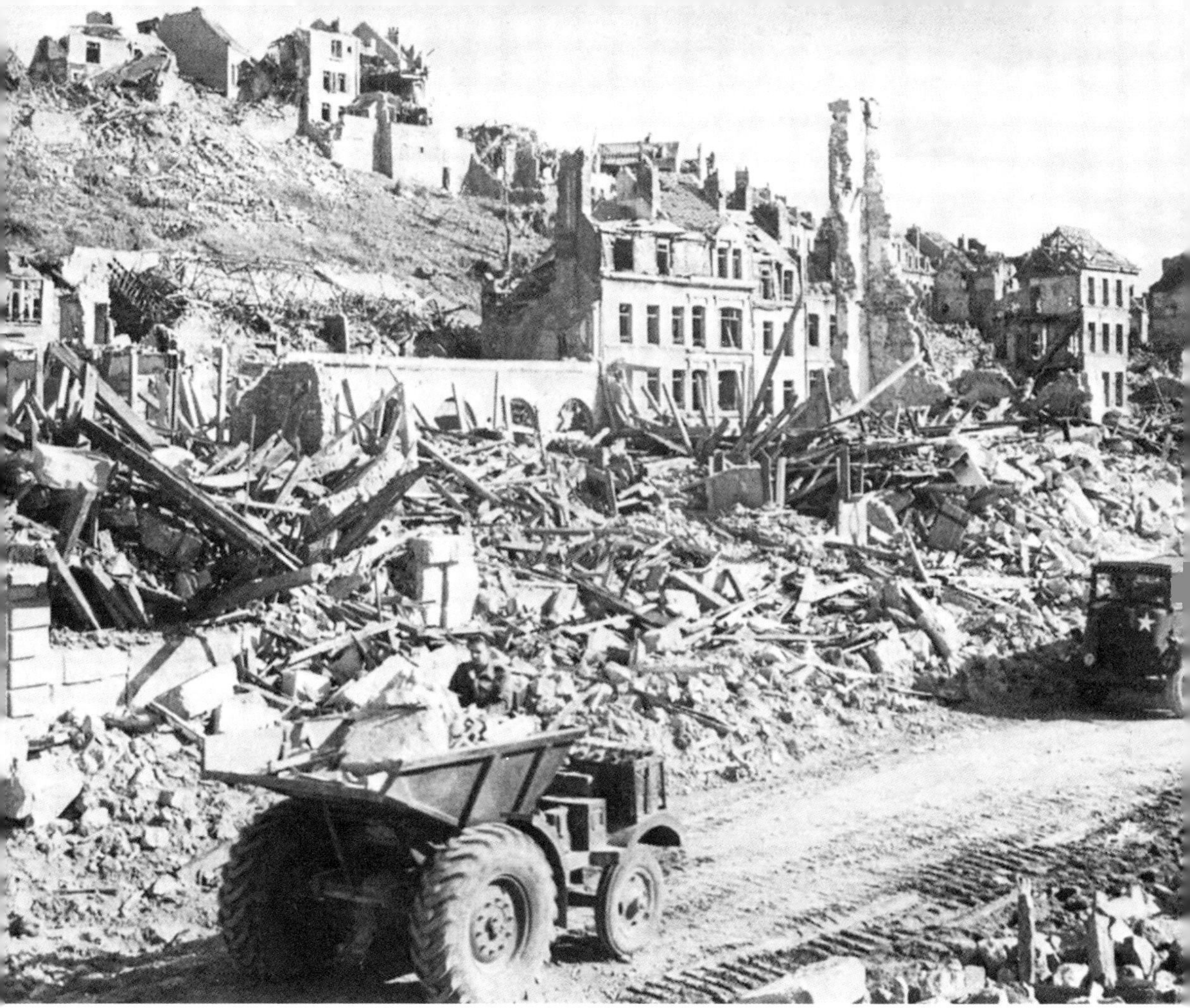

This is all that remained of the old Hôtel Folkestone on the Rue de Boston which runs just behind the Quai Gambetta. (IWM)

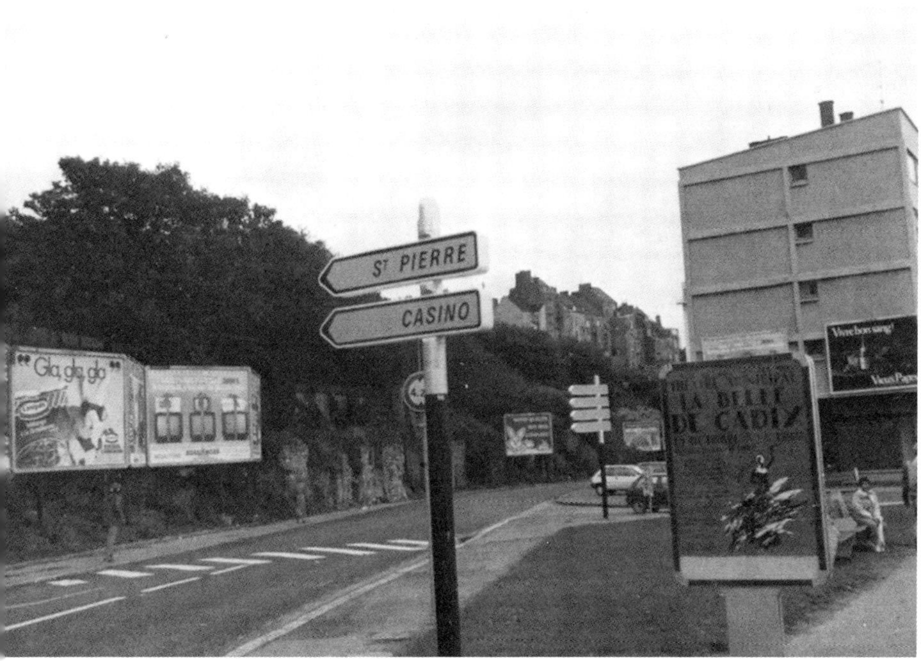
ST PIERRE
CASINO
LA BELLE
DE CADIX

Ruins remained in what became the Rue du Folkestone in the comparison from the 1990s, though today the area has been entirely redeveloped.

The port pictured by No. 542 Squadron on 25th September. Prominent in the top, centre the destroyed S-Boot pens.
(KEELE UNIVERSITY)

RADE CARNOT
TRAVERSE
R.C. OIL TANKS
40' DIA x 30' HIGH
CONCRETE RAMPS
OLD RAMPS
DIGUE DU LARGE
JETÉE SUD-OUEST
JETÉE NORD EST
COAL TRANSPORTERS
APPONTEMENT NORD
APPONTEMENT OUEST
BASSIN LOUBET
QUAI SUD
OIL TANKS DEMOLISHED
COVERED PENS
AVANT PORT
BRANCHE SUD
WOODEN PIERS
SLIPWAY
WOODEN PIER
EPERON DE LA GARE MARITIME
QUAI DES EXCURSIONNISTES
QUAI D'ECHOUAGE
LOCK
QUAI DE L'ESTAGE
QUAI NORD EST
GARE MARITIME
FLOATING DOCK
QUAI OUEST
BASSIN-A-FLOT
QUAI DE 150 M.
Q. DU LOUVRE
FISH MARKET
QUAI CHANZY
PORT DE MARÉE
STEPS
QUAI GAMBETTA
PONT
GRIDIRONG
MARGUET
CENTRAL
STATION
ARRIERE PORT
QUAI GAMBETTA
YARDS 100 0 100 200 300 400

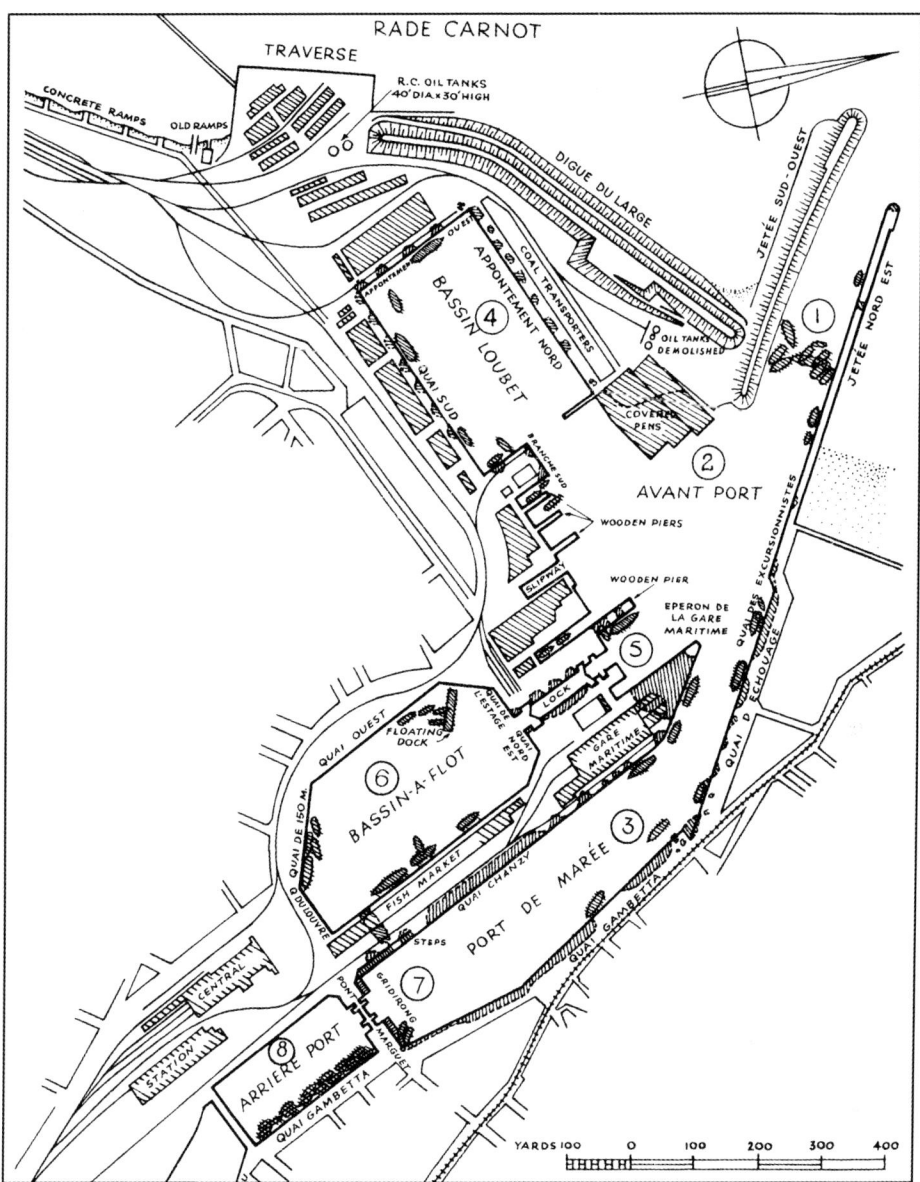

As the whole purpose of Operation 'Wellhit' was the capture of the port and its speedy rehabilitation, a Port Construction and Repair reconnaissance party was standing by, ready to enter the area as soon as it was reasonably safe to do so. The engineers went in on 20th September, while pockets of resistance were still active, and one officer of the reconnaissance party found himself pinned down all day by enemy fire and had to remain under cover till darkness fell. Demolitions were found to be thorough and extensive blocking by wrecks had been carried out. The general situation they found was as follows (numbers refer to plan): 1 - Entrance Channel mined and blocked with sunken craft. 2 - Avant Port mined, but no obstructions. 3 - Port de Marée. No sunk craft. Quays completely demolished and cranes wrecked. 4 - Bassin Loubet. Some craft sunk against quays. Reinforced concrete piled quay, Appontement Nord, breached in nine places, but could be bridged. Appontement Quest too badly damaged for repair. Quai Sud breached in seven places but repairable. All buildings wrecked. 5 - Locks to Bassin à Flot. Badly damaged and obstructed by debris; inner gates demolished; outer gates in open position; operating machinery wrecked. 6 - Bassin à Flot. Craft sunk in three groups, leaving considerable lengths of quay unobstructed. Only one crater in quays. 7 - Locks to Arrière Port. Lock gates in order and holding water, but approach obstructed by silt and rubble. 8 - Arrière Port. Quays intact, but Quai Gambetta obstructed by numerous sunk vessels.

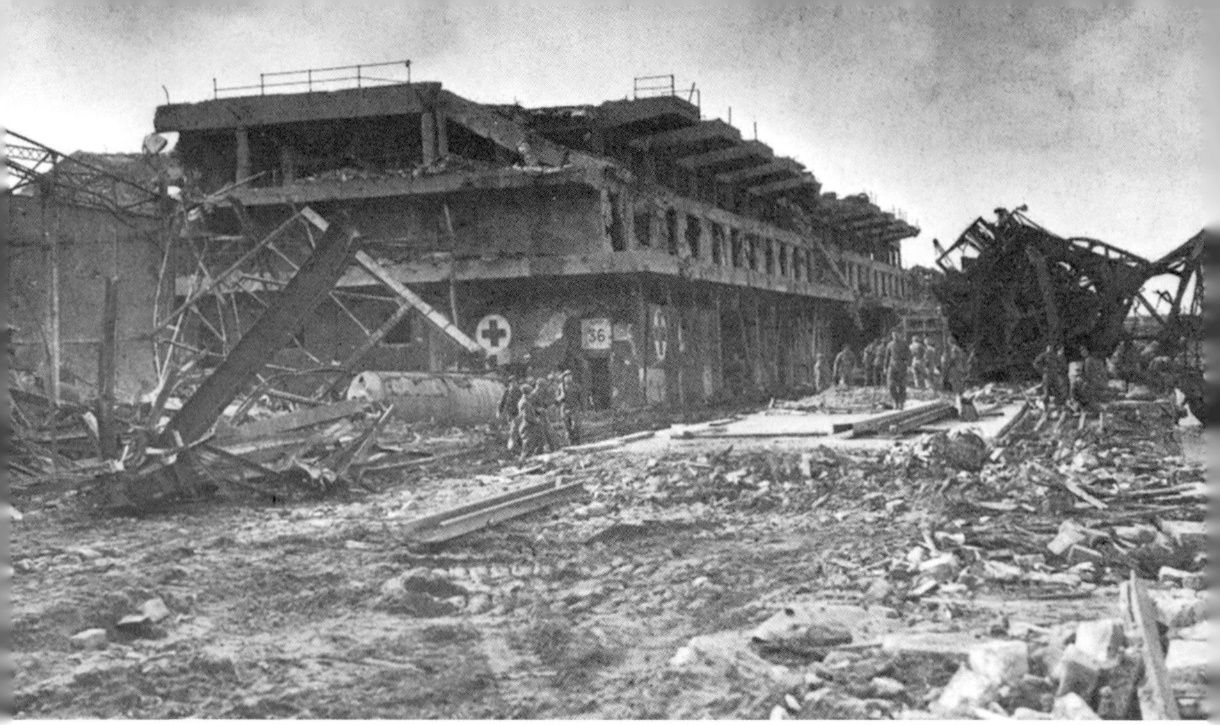

As a result of the reconnaissance, a short-term reinstatement plan was drawn up to repair and provide access to the most promising lengths of quay. These were the Quai Sud and Appontement Nord in Bassin Loubet; the Quai des Excursionnistes and Quai d'Echouage in the Avant Port; and the Quai Gambetta and Quai Gare Maritime in the Port de Marée. At the same time, the outer lock gates to the Bassin à Flot were to be repaired. The work was allocated to the Royal Engineers' No. 2 Port Reconstruction and Repair Group under Lieutenant-Colonel C. P. Shellbourne, embodying Nos. 935 and 937 Port Construction and Repair Companies supported by No. 238 Company, Pioneer Corps, and No. 44 Mechanical Equipment (Transportation) Section. Work continued for the next three months employing over 300,000 man-hours of labour with another 20,000 plant-hours of heavy equipment. Materials totalled 1,142 tons of cement, 7,137 tons of ballast, 10,000 linear feet of piling and a similar amount of RSJs, and 170,000 feet of steel reinforcement. (IWM)

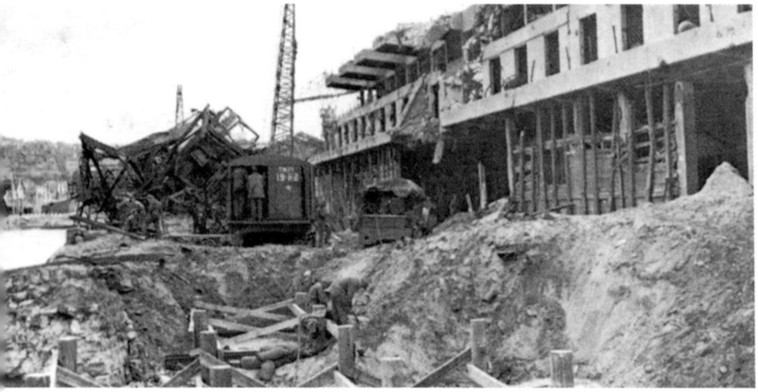

Priority was given to the repairs in the Bassin Loubet, as the Quai Sud offered the deepest water in the port (28 feet). Here, heavy timber piles have been sunk in one of the craters and cross-braced ready to receive the horizontal beams which had to be improvised by welding together two sections of steel piling to form a box-section. Steel troughing was then placed on top of this and concreted to form the new roadway. Repair of the Quai Sud was started on 26th September and completed four days later, having absorbed a total of 60,000 man-hours. (IWM)

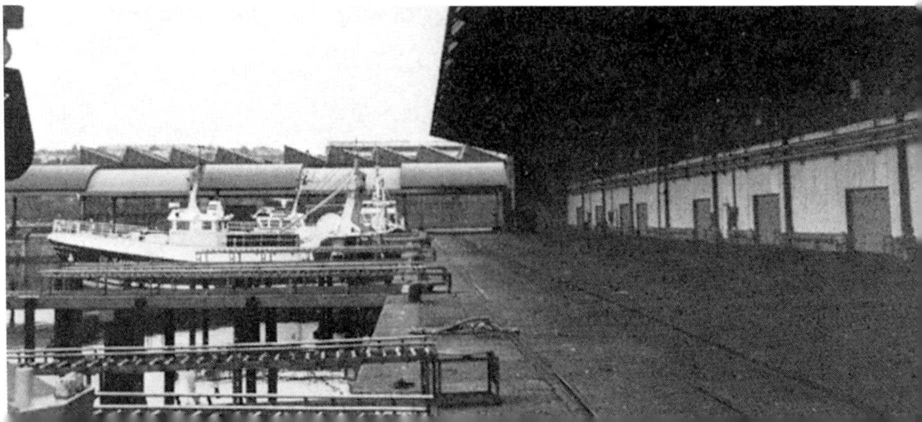

Today, a Nouvelle Halle, constructed for the Boulogne fishing fleet, stands on the quayside.

While the Royal Engineers commenced working on the repair of the quays, the Royal Navy began assisting in minesweeping and salvage in the harbour itself, priority being given to the removal of the sunken ships in the entrance channel. Although explosives were used to try to disperse the wrecks, it proved a very difficult task; so much so that it looked as if the quays might be finished before the berths alongside were cleared. Urgent attention was therefore also given to opening up the Bassin à Flot which could yield undamaged quays, even though it could only offer a 21-ft depth, as soon as the lock gates could be repaired. Work began on 3rd October and was about half complete

when the coaster Guernsey Queen struck a mine right outside the lock, completely blocking the entrance. Even though extra help was rushed in by the Port Construction and Repair troops, the wreck was not cleared until 20th November. Parallel with the mine and wreck clearance and the rebuilding of the quays in the Bassin Loubet, work began on the Quai des Excursionnistes, Quai d'Echouage and Quai Gambetta. Although the water depth was less, these quays offered a fairly quick solution for berths for coasters and personnel ships. Three breaches were repaired by renewing the columns and beams, covering the gaps with steel sheet piling used as troughing, and casting a new slab which was then paved flush with the existing roadway. However, the work still took several weeks and the three quays were not completed until 4th November, by which time Ostend was coming on stream and Antwerp was offering the prospect of unlimited facilities. (IWM)

The same vantage point in 1994.

Operation 'Wellhit' • 117

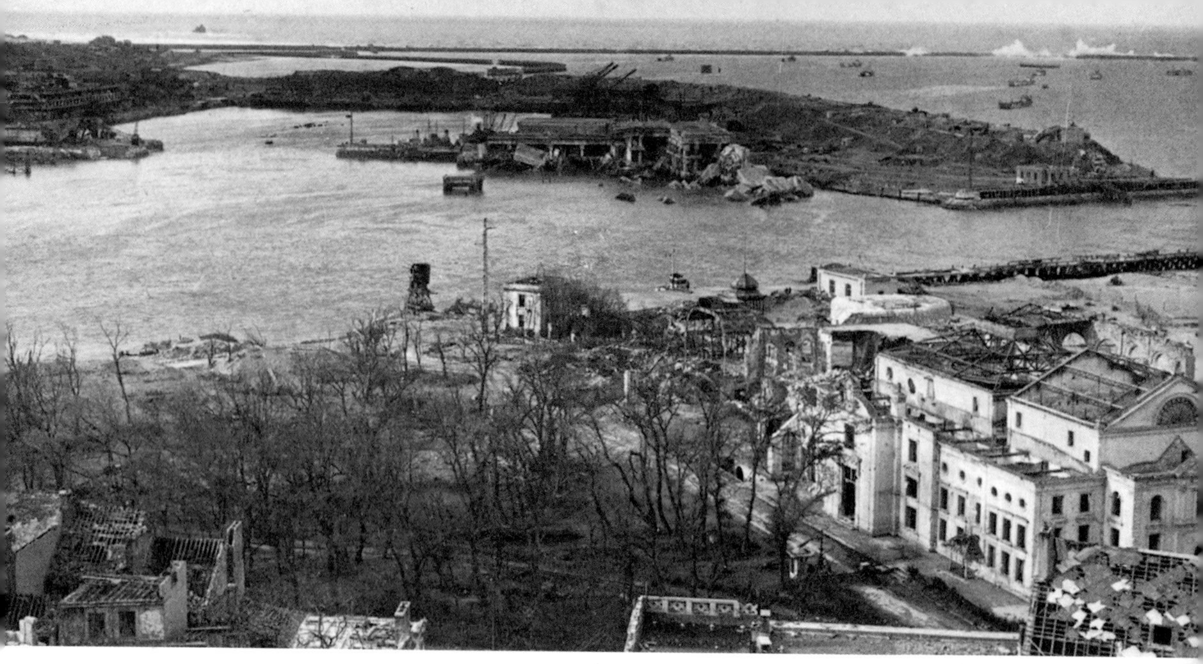

In this view, we are looking north-west past the Casino towards the S-Boot pens at the entrance to Bassin Loubet. (IWM)

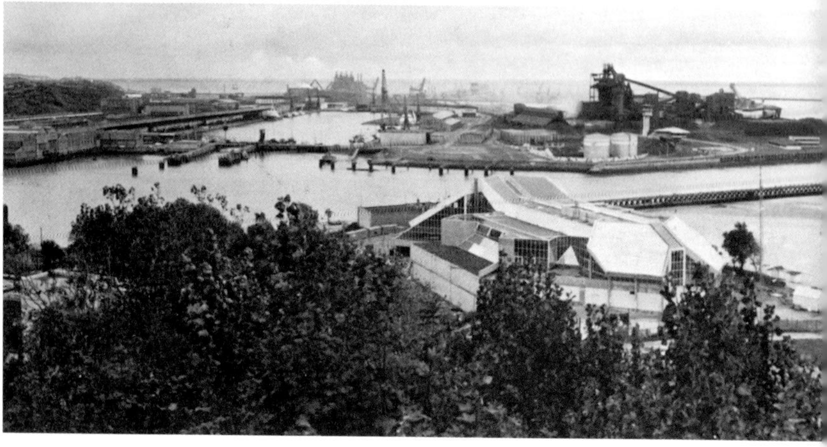

Today the Casino has been rebuilt and the pens demolished. The picture was taken from the fire control bunker.

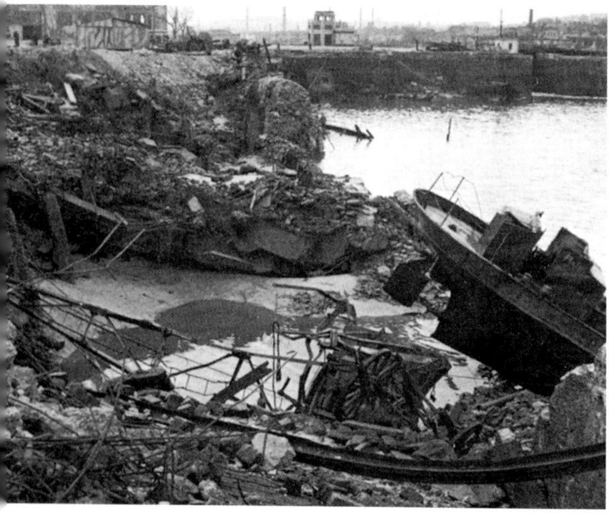

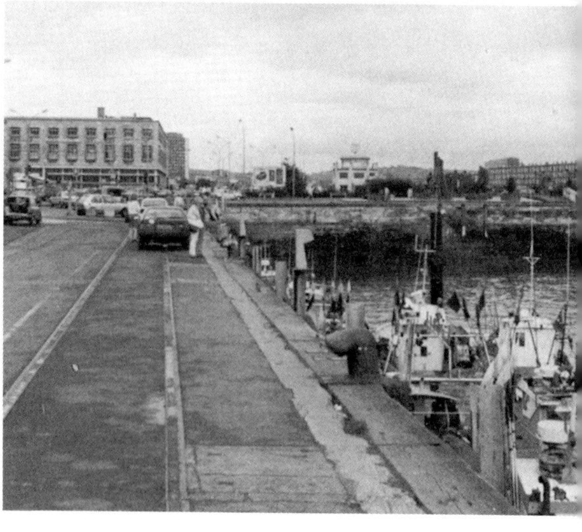

The condition of the Bassin Loubet - 1944 and 1994.

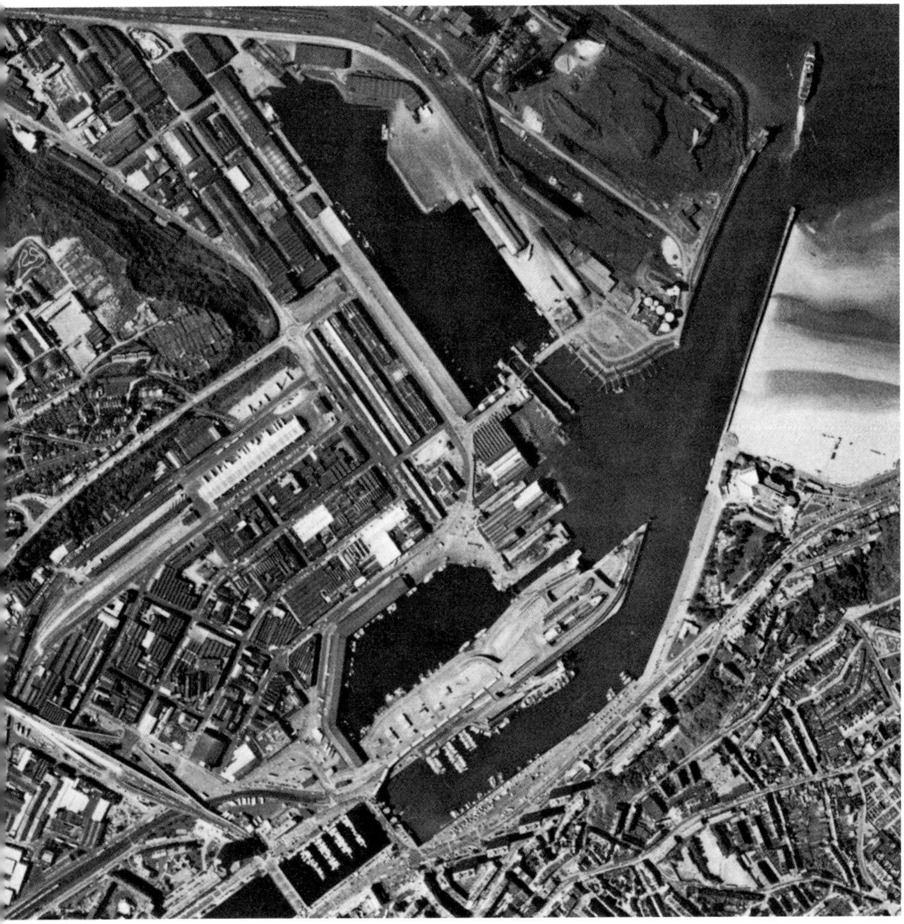

Antwerp received its first convoy on 28th November, effecting a complete revolution for the supply-starved Allied armies. Boulogne, along with Dieppe, Ostend and Calais, then took on a lesser rôle as British-occupied ports, along with the American operated Le Havre, Rouen and Cherbourg. After the war, Boulogne re-established its commercial activities although its traditional position as one of the main entry ports for France was curtailed in 1993 when the cross-Channel passenger ferry link with Folkestone was withdrawn. Compare this 1993 picture with the 1945 shot on page 114. (IGN)

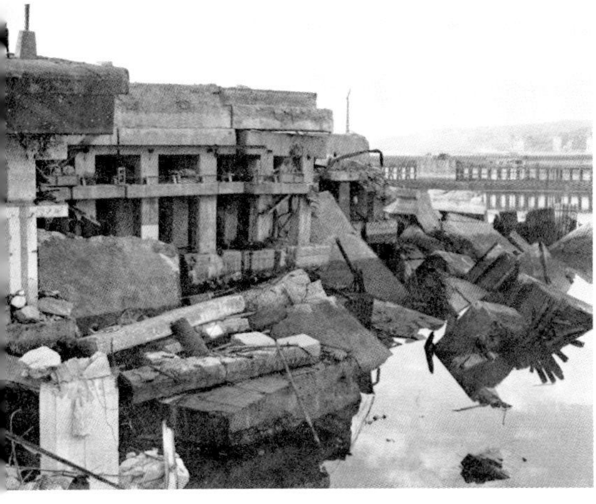

One structure not subject to RE repairs was the S-Boot shelter which had been built at the southern end of the Appontement Nord. Its reinforced concrete roof was 12 feet thick, though this had been partially demolished. (IWM)

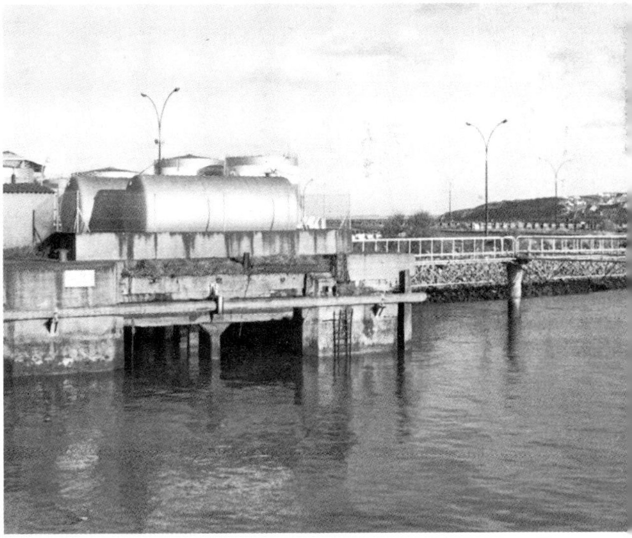

A small section remained visible in 1994 though further development has since continued to subsume traces of the past.

The enemy force had been only a little smaller than that at Le Havre, and the two Canadian brigades engaged against it had lost more men than the two British divisions committed to taking the larger city. In view of the strength of the ground and the defences, it was fortunate, as an observer said, that the enemy's will to fight was not stronger. The German defenders frequently went on firing until the Canadian infantry were close to their positions, and then gave themselves up, in many cases having their kit packed ready to surrender.

It was the German artillery that caused most of the Canadian losses, and it is evident that the neutralisation of enemy batteries was less effective than at Le Havre. The efforts of bomber command were more limited than that undertaken at Le Havre, though other factors also came into play. Naval bombardment was impractical due to the presence of extremely powerful German coastal batteries in the Pas-de-Calais. Also, shortages of shells prevented a full artillery counter-battery programme being undertaken before the actual day of the assault. A Canadian artillery commentary on the first day's fighting attributed the failure to silence some batteries partly to the lightness of the concentrations used, 'seldom more than 2 [guns] to 1', and partly to the exceptionally strong construction of the enemy gun positions. Operational researchers estimated in one case, that of a battery of six 8.8cm guns at Honriville south of the harbour, that the artillery put down 5,700 rounds on it within a circle 300 yards in diameter, but the battery nevertheless continued in action and themselves fired some 2,000 rounds. The same investigators found deficiencies in Canadian artillery intelligence. Lists compiled showing hostile battery locations before the operation were found to contain some dummy positions, on which bombs and shells were wasted, while some actual batteries were omitted. Eight previously unknown batteries were reported in action on 17th September.

Boulogne had offered the hope of a considerable improvement in the Allies' administrative situation. Though not a major harbour, it had a total seaborne cargo movement, inward and outward, of over a million tons in 1937 and was considered 'the first fishing port of France'. Unfortunately, however, the harbour installations had been extensively damaged by the enemy's demolitions and by bombing during the attack or earlier. Several ships had been sunk across the harbour mouth, most of the cranes had been destroyed and the locks damaged. Consequently, the port only begun to be brought into use on 12th October, and so there was no immediate alleviation of the Allied supply problem.

AFTERMATH

BETWEEN 16TH AND 30TH SEPTEMBER, Canadian 3rd Division, once again supported by elements of 79th Armoured Division, attacked Calais during Operation Undergo. The pattern of the attack followed that on Boulogne but progress was more tentative. First the Channel batteries around Cap Gris Nez failed to be taken, then the main attack on the town bogged down. In the end a truce was held on 28th September during which 20,000 inhabitants were evacuated, The Germans capitulated in short order once the attack was resumed. By this point, Montgomery had lost faith with Crerar's method of conducting operations, which he described as 'badly handled and slow.' It has been suggested that Crerar's subsequent 'sick leave' was more of a convenient cover for replacing him with Guy Simonds in whom Monty had greater confidence.

Dunkirk was judged too small to warrant the risk of an attack and so instead the town was besieged and left in the hands of its garrison. Initially Canadian 2nd Division, followed by the 1st Czechoslovakian Armoured Brigade were charged with maintaining the siege. Despite occasional harrying attacks, little effort was made to capture the town. In the end, the garrison were able to hold out until 9th May 1945 – the day after the formal surrender of Nazi Germany.

THE CONTROVERSY

THE PRIMARY IMPERATIVE of an army commander is to achieve strategic goals whilst incurring the fewest casualties possible. In order to achieve this aim, it is essential to use whatever means are available and to innovate by exploring whatever new resource is presented. In the summer of 1944, the latest innovation was the use of the strategic bomber force in order to minimise losses to the assaulting troops when attacking prepared positions.

Even by September of 1944 the results of this method were, at best, ambiguous. At Monte Cassino, Italy, an ancient monastery that overlooked a plain over which the Allies required egress was bombed to rubble'. The ruins thereafter provided ideal cover for the defending German force, from which they were able to hold against rigorous ground attacks. Further experimentation took place during the campaign in Normandy. In order to protect the right flank of Operation Epsom at the end of June, the town of Villers-Bocage was targeted by a force of Lancaster bombers in daylight. As a hub of the road network, west of the battlefield, there was clearly an imperative to deny the town to the enemy. Though it was presumed to be largely evacuated, there were still a number of civilians who had decided to ride out the fighting in the hope of protecting their homes. The town was severely damaged though the goal of preventing its use to the enemy was broadly successful. It was more by luck than judgement that many of the remaining townspeople had taken shelter in the Chateau, which was being used as a hospital for those unable to escape. Miraculously, it remained untouched. However, the town was not entirely deserted and so a terrible cost was paid by those civilians who had remained behind. Caen too suffered grievous bombing, turning much of the ancient city into smoking heaps of rubble interspersed with the skeletal remains of buildings. As with Monte Cassino, the piled rubble proved invaluable to the German defence and made its capture all the more difficult. An estimated 1,150 civilians had been killed by the bombing of Caen and a further 3,000 wounded. The next major effort was the innovative use of the bomber force to beat the ground in front of a massed tank assault – Operation Goodwood. Whilst it did pulverise German troops unlucky enough to find themselves within the target area, reinforcements were quickly able to infiltrate the space after the bombers had passed and their resistance, combined with the damage to roads and infrastructure caused by the bombing, meant that the attack bogged down and did not achieve its hoped-for breakthrough. Worse was to follow in the US sector when the US 8th Army Air Force was used to kick off operation Cobra. A bomb-line was selected that ran parallel to the front line with what seemed a generous separation between the target and the forward troops. Indeed, the first wave of the bomber force were able to accurately drop their bombs in the target area and the following stream of bombers simply had to drop their bombs on the pall of smoke created by the bombs of the preceding aircraft. What nobody seems to have anticipated was that a southerly wind was carrying that smoke towards their own lines. Catastrophically, bombs began to fall on the forward positions of the troops waiting to make the attack. The Americans suffered 600 casualties, 111 of whom were killed, including Lieutenant General Leslie McNair, who had ventured forward to watch the spectacle that the bombing presented. Of these five bombing attacks that preceded the assaults on Le Havre and Boulogne, only one had garnered a clear military benefit for the Allies. It is perhaps surprising that bombing remained the preferred solution for quelling the defences, when artillery could be called on to provide much more targeted support.

With any new method there is a learning process. It may be judged that unanticipated factors overly affected the outcomes and that, once absorbed, the lessons could be applied to the next attempt resulting in the hoped-for 'easy' advance. There were aspects of each of these experiments which might suggest that detail changes to the plan might offer a solution and this proved too great a temptation for commanders intent on minimising ground losses to their own side.

Decisions on the use of the bomber force were not taken lightly. Commanders were in an invidious position, weighing the imperatives of a quick victory where troop losses would be diminished and vital supply ports could be opened against the resultant civilian loss of life. In the case of both Le Havre and Boulogne the large civilian populations were effectively trapped, whilst delaying operations meant that there would be more time for the Germans to strengthen defences. Naturally, there is a desire to avoid civilian casualties, particularly when they are those of an ally but by the fifth year of the war the desire to get the job done, as swiftly as possible, outweighed other considerations. In one measure this was regarded as the price of liberation.

Bringing us back to the preparation for the assault on Le Havre, the dilemma came to a head in the late afternoon of 3rd September when the means of supporting the attack were being weighed. Major-General Evelyn 'Bubbles' Barker, the 49th Division commander,

In the early evening of 3rd September, three German envoys entered the British lines under a white flag to discuss the terms of the surrender ultimatum addressed to the Le Havre garrison by the British besiegers. The negotiations took place at the villa (left) of the former Mayor of Gonfréville on the Route Nationale 14 (today the D6015), the main road east out of Le Havre. (EDDY FLORENTIN)

The picture was taken at 0900 on the morning of the 4th, when the delegates returned to the house with Oberst Wildermuth's written reply. The latter flatly rejected the British demand of unconditional surrender, whereupon General John Crocker, the British I Corps commander, refused Wildermuth's request to allow the civilian population to evacuate from the besieged and bomb-threatened city. The breakdown of negotiations sealed the fate of Le Havre and its cornered population, as destruction by naval and aerial bombardment prior to an assault was now inevitable. (DANIEL PALFREY)

declared an 11-hour truce — from 7 p.m. till 6 a.m. — to enable him to send an ultimatum to the Germans. At 1900-hrs, Brigadier John Walker, commander of the 146th Brigade, approached the German lines in an armoured car carrying a white flag and a loudspeaker and invited the enemy to send a representative to receive terms of surrender. Shortly afterwards, three German envoys — a Leutnant and two NCOs — entered the British lines where they were informed of the British terms: unconditional surrender or else intensive air and naval bombardment would ensue. The Germans took the ultimatum back into Le Havre and early on the 4th returned with a letter from Oberst Wildermuth in which he refused to surrender but instead asked for a two-day armistice to evacuate the civilians. Wildermuth's answer was clearly dictated by the direct order given to him when he took command of the Festung, compelling him to hold to the last man. The German offer to evacuate the French population and thereby allow an opportunity to avoid suffering severe casualties was referred back to General Crocker, who refused. His decision was on the grounds that there was 'no time' — a refusal that sealed the fate of those living in Le Havre and has been the source of much controversy and debate ever since, especially in France. Crockers uncompromising stance was clearly based on the pressure he was under to attempt to alleviate the dire supply situation and prevent the Germans time to improve their defences or to start demolishing the port.

In a last gasp attempt to spare further damage and save the lives of soldiers and civilians, some 922,000 'safe conduct' leaflets were dropped by aircraft or fired into the city by gunners appealing to the German soldiers to surrender. Loudspeaker teams addressed the same message to the German forward defence lines. All to little avail.

Whilst the decision faced by the top brass allowed the ends to justify the means, those charged with the execution of the orders

Newspaper reports detailing Douglas-Home's treatment by the British press. Whilst he clearly had a rough ride from the reading public, it is perhaps heartening that such a letter could be considered suitable as a feature. It seems quite unlikely that similar sentiments would have been published under the Nazi regime.

The Controversy • 125

were not necessarily comfortable with what they were called on to do. The moral dilemma was played out in one specific public episode, though it surely rankled in the minds of airmen and soldiers alike. The episode was the extraordinary affair of Captain William Douglas-Home, a subaltern serving in C Squadron, 141st RAC, who objected to what he saw as the unnecessary bombing of a town still inhabited by civilians. He considered his orders a war crime, and therefore refused to go into action. A member of an aristocratic family, educated at Eton and Oxford (his eldest brother Alec would become Prime Minister in 1963), Douglas-Home had in 1941-43 unsuccessfully contested three parliamentary by-elections as an independent candidate opposed to the Allies' war aim of unconditional surrender. Sent to France with his regiment, he had seen the result of the bombing of civilians at Caen, which deeply disturbed him, and on 30th August had written an open letter to the *Maidenhead Advertiser* repeating his criticism on the conduct of the war. On 5th September, assigned to act as liaison officer between his unit and the 51st Division for 'Astonia' and having heard that Oberst Wildermuth's offer to evacuate the French civilians had been rejected on the grounds that there was 'no time', Douglas-Home went to his battalion commander, Lieutenant-Colonel Herbert Waddell, and told him that he refused to take part in the operation, as his conscience would not allow it. Waddell called a witness and gave Douglas-Home a direct order, which he refused. Waddell initially did nothing with Douglas-Home's disobedience but sent him back to his squadron. Two weeks later, at Boulogne, Douglas-Home made another stand when he offered to go down into the besieged port and negotiate a surrender with the Germans. By now, Waddell had decided his subordinate's defiance at Le Havre could not be tolerated and put him under arrest to be court-martialled. (His hesitation had repercussions for Waddell too, for it caused him to be relieved of his command a few weeks later). At Douglas-Home's trial, held in Belgium on 25th October, it became clear that his refusal was symbolic and that he had done it to draw public attention to the moral issue of bombing civilians and to the unnecessary waste of lives brought about by the unconditional surrender policy. Douglas-Home argued that a man's conscience came before orders which he believed to be morally wrong. The court did not accept this and sentenced him to dishonourable discharge and 12 months of hard labour (of which he served eight at Wormwood Scrubs and Wakefield Prison).

Although Douglas-Home was publicly scorned at the time, ironically, at the later Nuremberg trials, Allied judges would condemn German officers for failing to do exactly what he had done: refusing to obey orders which they knew to be morally wrong. This obvious double standard always bothered Douglas-Home. In 1988, after Britain had condemned former UN Secretary-General Kurt Waldheim for not refusing wartime orders that he knew to be ethically wrong, Douglas-Home (who after the war had become a well-known playwright) sought to get his honour restored and applied for his case to be reconsidered. The War Office declined to re-open the case and in 1991 he abandoned his appeal. He died on 28th September 1992.

Whilst his views did not chime with the majority, they did reflect an undercurrent of opinion that questioned the lengths to which the war could be pursued.

CONCLUSION

THE USE OF THE STRATEGIC BOMBING FORCE has, as detailed, remained controversial. The diversion of heavy bombers away from their more normal industrial targets in Germany, the questionable results of the bombing, cratering the combat area, and most particularly the unavoidable loss of civilian lives were a strong indication that their use was ill-thought through. The clear irony was that the very means by which the Allies were able to force a rapid entry into the ports – the bombing – had a considerable hand in rendering them useless in the short-term easement of the supply crisis.

Air Marshall Sir Arthur Coningham was certainly unhappy with the use of resources and concluded that the part played by Air Vice Marshall Leslie Brown, commanding 84 Group RAF had been too 'subservient' to the wishes of the Army. As a consequence, he was sacked and replaced by Air Vice Marshall Edmund Hudlestone.

With Le Havre being assigned to the Americans as a logistic hub, engineer troops of the US 351st, 373rd and 392nd Engineer General Service Regiments, the 1055th and 1061st Port Construction and Repair Groups, the 577th Dump Truck Company, 1593rd Utilities Detachment, and two companies of British marine engineers arrived to restore the

The centre of Le Havre reduced to rubble by the British aerial bombing. In all, the port had suffered 117 Allied raids during the war, of which those immediately preceding 'Astonia' were the heaviest. Noteworthy among those raids was that staged by 617 Squadron on 13th June 1944 when Tallboy 'earthquake' bombs were used to destroy the Schnellboot bunker in the dock. In all, the bombing left over 80 per cent of the city in ruins. Some 10,000 homes had been destroyed, as well as countless public buildings, five churches, two hospitals, 34 primary schools — the list is endless. A total of 5,126 citizens had been killed and 31,000 made homeless. (PORT AUTONOME DU HAVRE)

The memorial commemorating the assault on Le Havre is shown as it looked in 2003, pictured from 25,000 feet. Montivilliers has grown since the war and the terrain of Lanes 10 and 11 is now covered by modern housing enclosed on the west by a new bypass, but the ground over which the other lanes ran largely remains open farmland, much as it was in 1944. The small road that was Lane 8 still runs south from the D52. The wooded square that formed German Strongpoint 5 — the target of Lanes 4 to 6 — clearly stands out, as does the wooded valley at bottom left that was part of Strongpoint 8. The Astonia Memorial stands on the D52, just below the point where the 'Rum' team crossed the anti-tank ditch. (IGN 2003fd76/25000C32)

harbour facilities and open up the ocean port to American shipping. They began by clearing the beaches of mines, allowing landing ships and craft to disembark troops and matériel on them. However, the Americans found the port itself so thoroughly mined and demolished by the Germans and so badly damaged by Allied bombing that Liberty ships could not use it until 9th October. Even then its capacity fell much below expectations. The heavy equipment and transport carried in American transatlantic Liberty ships were all packed in heavy crates, which could only be lifted by powerful dockside cranes, but at Le Havre these cranes had all been put out of action by the Germans. Thus, this boxed equipment had to be landed in Britain, then ferried across the Channel unpacked. By the end of October Le Havre was handling just 5,000 tons daily. Though this tonnage slowly increased, its contribution continued to fall short. Nevertheless, it continued to supply American forces until the end of the war.

Boulogne also had Port and Construction units allocated in order to attempt to clear the facilities so that it could accept shipping. A PLUTO[1] pipeline was laid from Dungeness in Kent to Boulogne and

---

[1] Pipe-Line Under The Ocean

begun to pump fuel on 8th October. The first ship to arrive in the docks did not unload until 14th October.

To add to their frustration, though Antwerp was liberated on 4th September, and the port captured largely intact thanks to the intervention of the Belgian resistance's 'White Brigade', the way to the sea remained barred. The Germans had fortified the Scheldt estuary, preventing access to shipping. The campaign to clear the Scheldt culminated in the amphibious landings on the island of Walcheren, which finally cleared the approaches to Antwerp on 8th November, though mine clearance meant that the first ships to reach the port did not arrive until 28th November.

It is worth noting that, after VE-Day, Le Havre was used as the main hub through which US troops were repatriated back home. By August 1946, some 3,675,000 soldiers had transited through the port.

The Astonia Memorial on the D52, the Montivilliers to Fontaine-la-Mallet road. Inaugurated in September 1994, it stands at a very appropriate spot, virtually on the start line of the assault by the armoured gapping teams on the German perimeter and with a clear view of former Strongpoint 5. It comprises a Churchill tank; a replica of an SBG bridge over a reconstructed section of the German anti-tank ditch; and a memorial decorated with information panels together with formation badges of the various British units involved in the Le Havre operation. The Churchill, aptly named Astonia, is adorned with tactical markings of several different formations: the bull's head of the 79th Armoured Division; the armoured glove and mace of the 34th Tank Brigade and the '156' unit code of the 147th RAC. The latter is a minor error since this armoured regiment, although belonging to the 34th Tank Brigade, did not take part in the Le Havre battle.

ORGANISATION TABLES

Key to organisation tables

An intrinsic element of the assaults on both Le Havre and Boulogne was the use of the specialised vehicles of 79th Armoured Division and its affiliated units. The Division was organised and used in quite a different way to more conventional units. In order to better understand how they could be employed, there follows a set of organisation tables that show the most common way in which they were used — as squadrons. The squadron is a throwback to the age of cavalry but is the equivalent of a company-sized formation in most armies. Typically this is a unit of between 120 and 200 all ranks including fighting, administration and supply elements. Three squadrons would be grouped to make a regiment in 'Armoured' units, or battalion in 'Tank' units — another peculiarity of British organisation as both represent a very similarly configured formation. The use of the squadron — or the half-squadron as was often the case — meant that the Division's resources could be spread across a number of engagements throughout the front line whilst maintaining its offensive potential.

One element that is underplayed in the diagrams is that of supply. There would be around thirty-five 3-ton lorries employed in the logistical arm of each squadron, which would clearly overwhelm the diagrams if they were included.

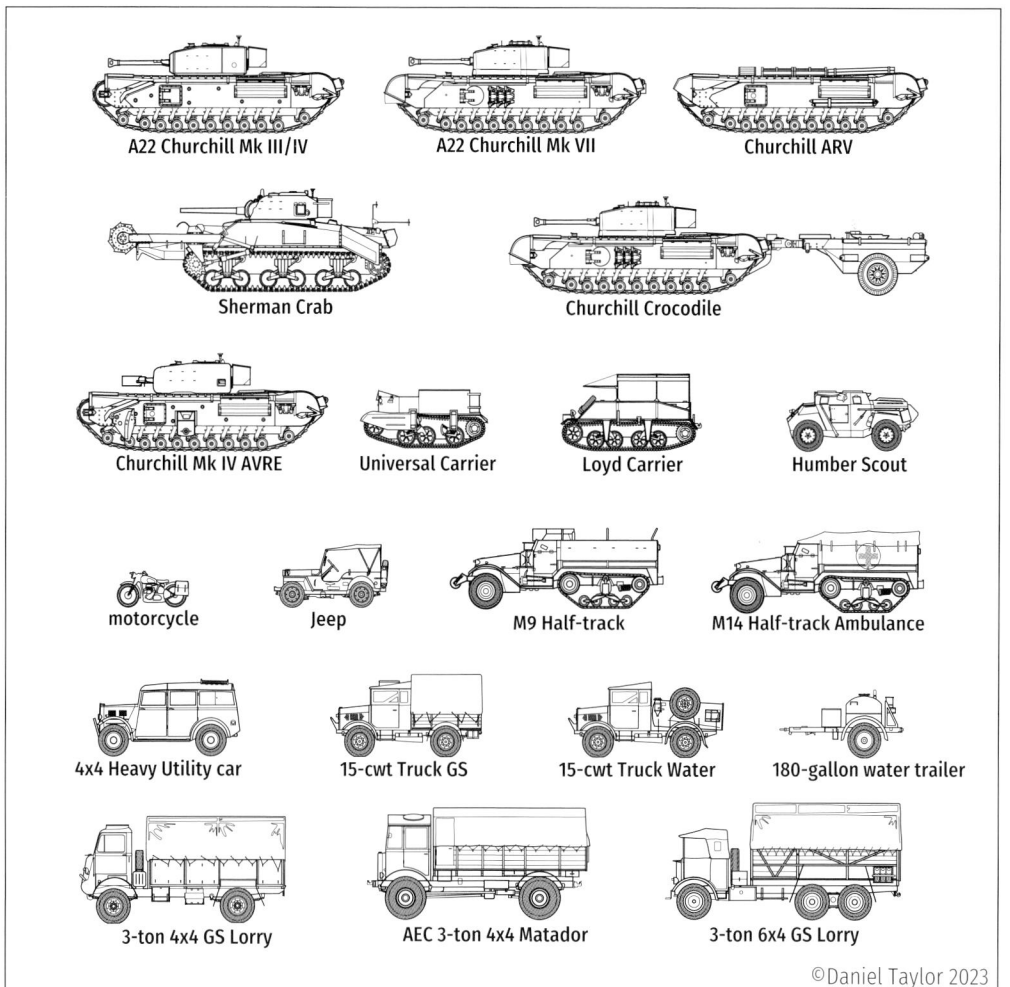

©Daniel Taylor 2023

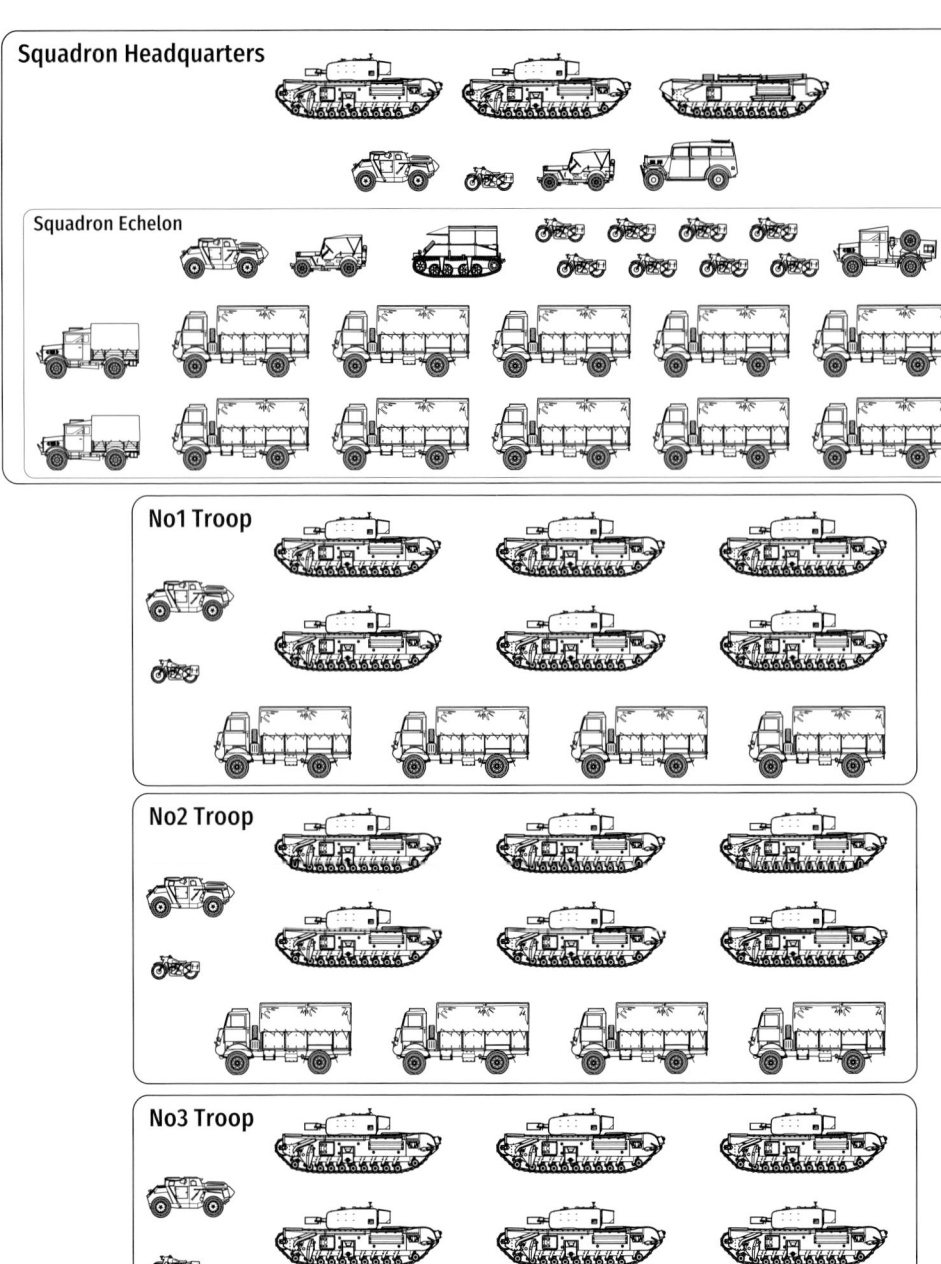

©Daniel Taylor 2023

Assault Squadron, Royal Engineers

An Assault Squadron Royal Engineers was designed to work independently of its regiment, supporting an infantry battalion for a task. As such, it adopted a much larger proportion of its parent regiment's transport than would be the case with most armoured units and each troop had its own embedded supply trucks. Each troop operated as two sections of three tanks. The squadron's primary function was to operate as engineers. Though they used modified Churchill tanks, they were not in any sense akin to armoured troops. Their role as assault engineers utilised their armoured vehicles to transport sappers and their equipment in order that they could carry out a variety of demolition tasks. The unit organisation had been changed in August 1944, reducing each squadron by one troop so that a training and supply echelon could be formed from these troops. This then provided replacement crews and equipment.

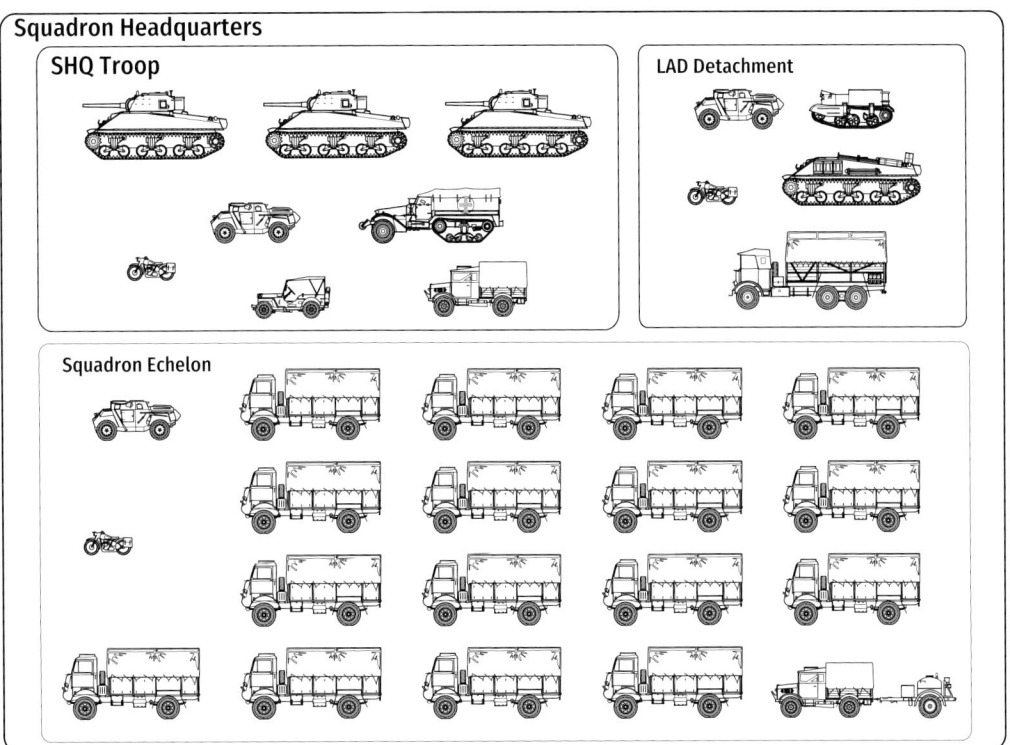

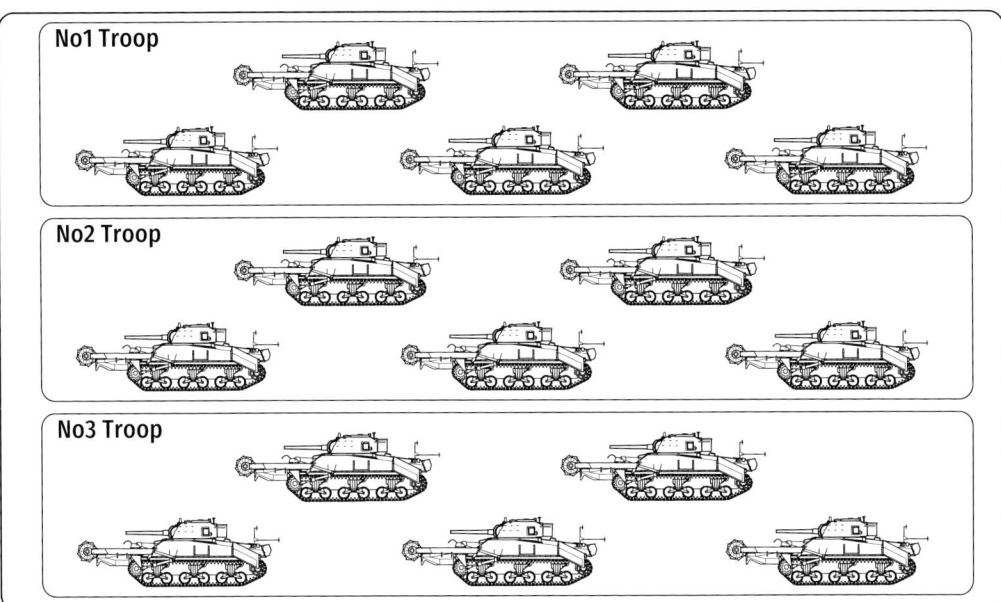

©Daniel Taylor 2023

Sherman Crab Squadron

Through the summer of 1944 30th Armoured Brigade was composed of three regiments each equipped with Sherman Crab tanks. After D-Day, it became normal for Crab units to deploy as individual squadrons in support of an infantry battalion in an attack, though dispositions could be modified to match circumstances. In action each troop would usually operate with three of their Crabs forward, clearing slightly overlapping lanes to give a gap approximately 24 feet wide through a minefield. The troop's other two flails would give fire support and be able to take over should those sweeping be incapacitated. Since the squadrons generally operated independently there was little need for regimental administrative services and these were largely devolved to each squadron by the parent regiment.

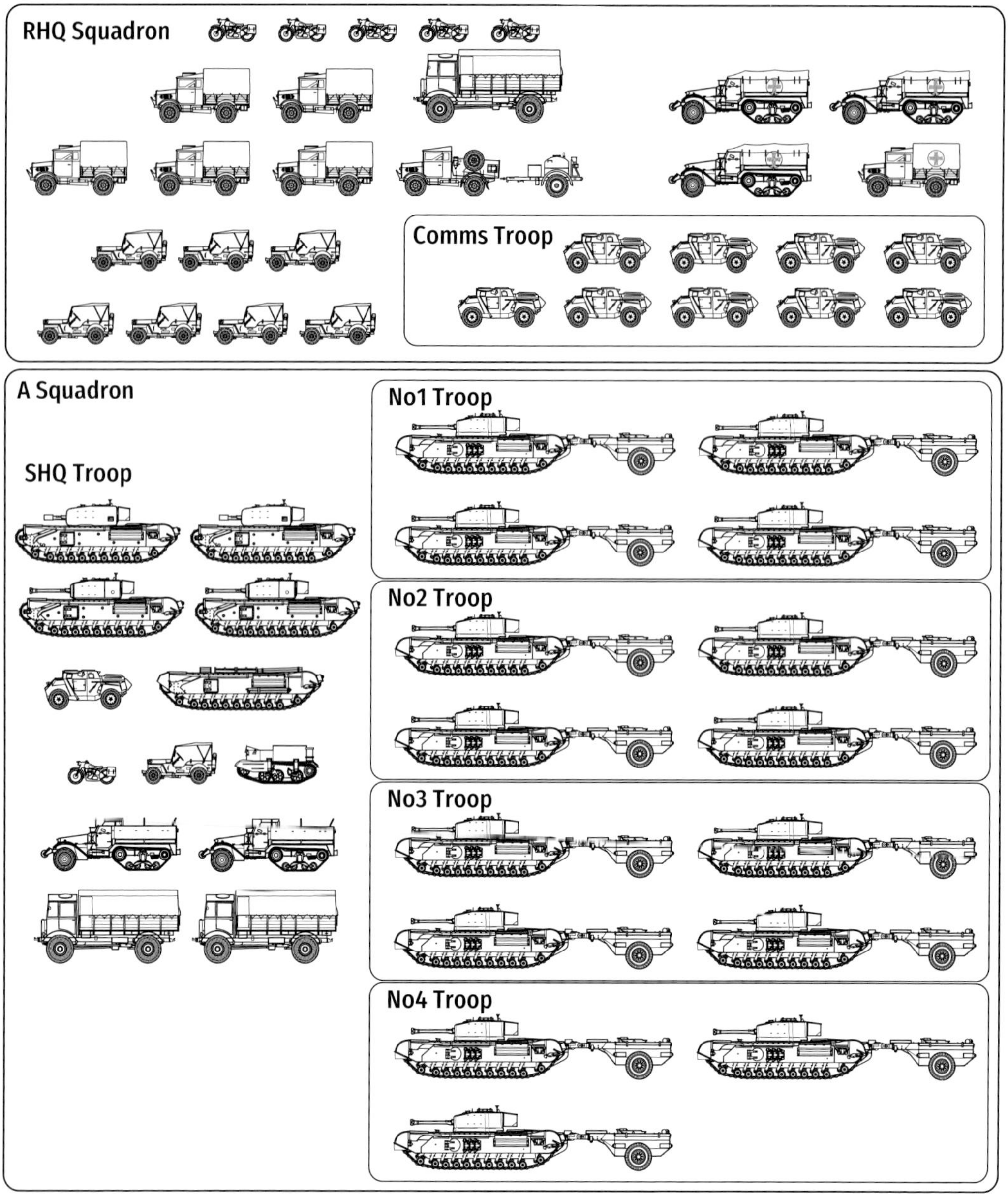
RHQ Squadron
Comms Troop
A Squadron
SHQ Troop
No1 Troop
No2 Troop
No3 Troop
No4 Troop

©Daniel Taylor 2023

Churchill Crocodile Tank Squadron

The tank battalions equipped with Crocodiles were organised in the same manner as other Infantry tank units. As such, at the conclusion of the Normandy campaign, the configuration was changed from five troops of three tanks per squadron to four troops of four (with the exception of the fourth troop as the number of tanks allocated had not increased). This change allowed them to operate as two half-squadrons, which was felt to be more tactically adaptable. As Crocodile units rarely operated as a whole battalion, much of the administration and supply was distributed between the three squadrons. Battalion headquarters control tanks were made available to the SHQs so that each half-squadron had one 75mm and one 95mm Close Support tank for command purposes.

The only unit operating Crocodiles at the time, 141 Battalion Royal Armoured Corps, had transferred to 79th Armoured Division from 31st Army Tank Brigade in July. This move permitted their employment in the same way that other 'Funnies' were used in support of attacks across the entire 21st Army Group front.

An unusual quirk of the Crocodile unit's echelon was that Medium Artillery Tractors replaced the more conventional 3-ton 4x4 trucks that equipped most armoured units. These were considered more suitable for working with and recovering the armoured trailers and would be used to tow the trailers when the unit was not in action. This was chiefly the AEC Matador, though the FWD SU COE and Mack NM 6 X 6 were also used. Though not illustrated here, each Crocodile squadron had 50 MATs rather than the 35 3-tonners usually allocated.

HOBART'S FUNNIES

Major General Percy Hobart, the 79th Armoured Division commander, organised and trained the division and his name became associated with the variety of vehicles they used.

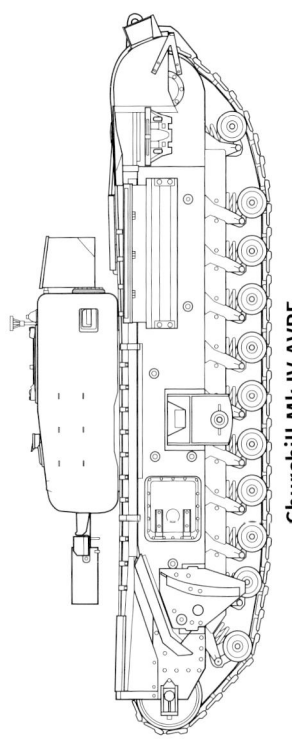

Churchill Mk IV AVRE

The AVRE was a conversion of the standard Churchill tank designed to support attacks on a variety of defensive positions. Its primary purpose was as a means of firing a 230mm Petard mortar, capable of defeating concrete bunkers. It had fittings that allowed it to be fitted with a variety of specialised equipment including the Small Box Girder bridge and fascines for crossing anti-tank ditches.

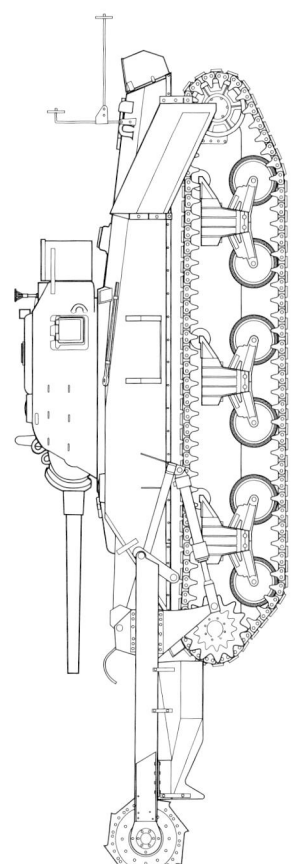

Sherman Mk V Crab

The abundance of Sherman tanks available to the Allies made it ideal as a basis for specialised armour. Probably the most successful of these conversions was the 'Crab', capable of beating a path through minefields and tearing apart barbed-wire entanglements.

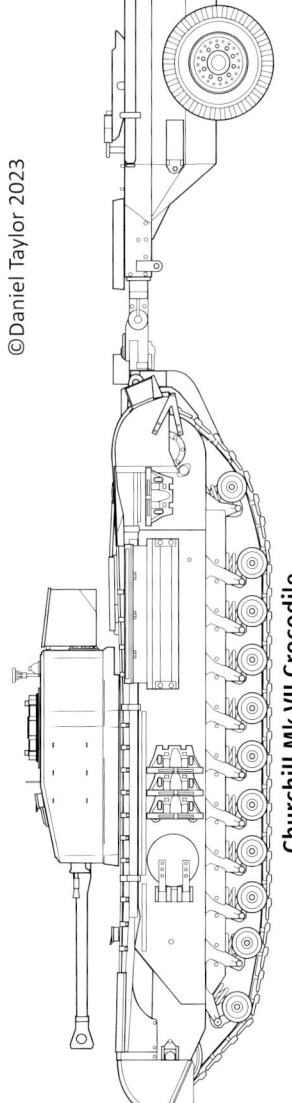

Churchill Mk VII Crocodile

Possibly the most feared tool in the Division's arsenal was the Churchill Crocodile flamethrower tank. Capable of projecting a flammable gel up to 150 metres, though 80 metres was more typical of its effective range. Its presence in an assault force was often enough to persuade the defenders to surrender. Crocodiles were operated by 141 Battalion, Royal Armoured Corps.

©Daniel Taylor 2023

The Funnies • 135

BIBLIOGRAPHY

Delaforce, P	*The Polar Bears: Monty's Left Flank*, Chancellor Press 1995. ISBN 978 0 7537 0265 9
Doherty, R	*Normandy 1944: The Road to Victory*, Spellmount. 2004 ISBN 978 1 86227 224 8
Ellis, Major L F	*Victory in the West: Volume I The Battle of Normandy,* London: HMSO 1962 ISBN 978 1 84574 058 0
Ellis, Major L F	*Victory in the West: Volume II The Defeat of Germany,* London: HMSO 1968 ISBN 978 1 84574 059 7
Fletcher, D	Vanguard of Victory, The 79th Armoured Division, London HMSO 1984 ISBN 0 11 290422 X
Montgomery, B L	*Normandy to the Baltic*, Hutchinson 1946 ISBN 978 818158 067 2
Hinsley, F H	*British Intelligence in the Second World War,* London HMSO 1993 ISBN 978 0 116309617
Saunders, H & Richards, D	*Royal Air Force 1939–45: Vol. III,* London: HMSO ISBN 978-0-11-771594-3
Shulman, M	*Defeat in the West, London,* Martin Secker & Warburg 1947 ISBN 978-0-304-36603-3
Stacey, C P & Bond, C C J	*The Victory Campaign: The operations in North-West Europe 1944–1945* QPCS Ottawa, 1960

A number of other documents and resources have been consulted including unit histories, reports and war establishment data in the British National Archive. We would also like to acknowledge the excellent resource collated by 'Trux' on unit organisation.